BRANDED ON MY ARM
AND IN MY SOUL

Branded on My Arm and in My Soul

A Holocaust Memoir

by

Abraham W. Landau

edited by

Joseph D. Thomas
Marsha L. McCabe
Jay Avila

published by

Spinner Publications, Inc.

New Bedford, Massachusetts

with

The Jewish Federation of Greater New Bedford

Library of Congress Cataloging-in-Publication Data

Landau, Abraham, 1922-2000.
  Branded on my arm and in my soul : a Holocaust memoir / edited by Joseph D. Thomas, Marsha L. McCabe, Jay Avila.
     p. cm.
  Includes bibliographical references and index.
  ISBN 978-0-932027-19-1 (pbk. : alk. paper) -- ISBN 978-0-932027-20-7 (hardcover : alk. paper)
1. Landau, Abraham, 1922-2000. 2. Jews--Poland--Wilczyn--Biography. 3. Holocaust, Jewish (1939-1945)--Poland--Personal narratives. 4. Wilczyn (Poland)--Biography. I. Thomas, Joseph D. II. McCabe, Marsha. III. Avila, Jay. IV. Title.
  DS134.72.L36A3 2011
  940.53'18092--dc23
  [B]
                                  2011032019

To My Loving Granddaughter, Lauren Joy

and

To the Children of the World

Donors

Liberation Donors *(Gifts of $5,000 or more)*

Mitzi & Warren Eisenberg Family Foundation

Massachusetts Humanities

Chai Donors *(Gifts of $2,500 ~ $4,000)*

John & Marsha Onufrak

Henry H. Crapo Charitable Trust

United Way of Greater New Bedford
Community Building Mini-Grants Program

Brigades Donors *(Gifts of $1,000 ~ $2,000)*

Dennis & Ann Kantor and Brian & Lauren Finger

New Bedford Arts Council

The Jewish Federation of Greater New Bedford

The Weinreb Berenda Carter Foundation

Paritsan Donors *(Gifts of $500 ~ $750)*

Alan & Ruth Ades Charitable Trust
William do Carmo & Family
Kenneth Lipman & Evelyn Baum
Zvi & Orna Landau & Family
Lorraine Rudnick
Barbara K. Samuels
Susan & Calvin Siegal
Dennis Skaliotis
Joseph & Catherine Winterhalter
Mel & Cynthia Yoken

Holocaust Remembrance Donors *(Gifts of $250 ~ $350)*

Jay Avila
Paul & Elaine Chervinsky
Michelle & Eric Colella
Ivan Dolowich
Sheldon & Shulamith Friedland
Kaufman, Dolowich, Voluck & Gonzo
Demarest Lloyd MacDonald
David Gilbertson & Carolee Matsumoto
Frederick A. Ryder
Jane & Joseph Thomas

Tikkum Olam Donors *(Gifts of $100 ~ $150)*

Emi Adachi
Deborah & Benjamin Baker
Chris & Janet Barnard
Peter & Joan Barney
Judith & Nate Barry
Joyce Goldstein Brink
Marcy & Sagi Brink-Danan & Family
Irene Buck
Dennis Leonard DeBell
Rachel B. Dressler
The Rev. Dr. Edward R. Dufresne
Amy Eisenberg
Barry Federman
Glaser Glass Corporation
Alexandra Harrison
Dina & Jeremy Harrison
Wil & Carole Herrup
Barbara Najjar & Jim Hijiya

David Jacobs
Sandra Jacobs
Rabbi Raphael Kanter
Mimi Elmer & Lyle Kantor
Sidney & Barbara Kaplan
Barbara & Norman Kaye
Stacy H. Kaye
Michele Koppelman
Maria T. Latour
Claire Levovsky
Rev. David A. Lima
Bettina Borders & Victor Mailey
Elizabeth P. Matahia
Martin M. Mazer
Mary Molino
Marianne Morrissey
Tom O'Connell
June Lynham Pina

Richard A. Pline
Judy Pollack
Anita & Leonard Poyant
Deborah Roher
Don Rudnick
Nathaniel Schudrich
Iris & Roger Slotkin
Sherrie Sobel
John D. Souza
Tifereth Israel Minyan Breakfast Club
Curt Waldbaum
Iris Wallace
John M. & Bonnie W. Werly
John Whoriskey, Jr
James F. Wilcox
David & Dara Yoken
Jonathan & Jody Yoken

Tolerance Donors *(Gifts of $50 ~ $60)*

Adam Abraham
Barbara Azizo
Ivy Feuerstadt & Barry Becken
Lucy Alexandria Bly
Cathy Breitman
Nancy Brown
Daniel & Linda Bryant
Betty Cambra
Deborah Cangemi
Nancy Cappelloni
Tom & Connie Carr
Dartmouth Tailor & Sue Chouinard
Shaun Connell
Elaine & Bobby Cowley
Kristine Daniels
Maureen Deneault
Jennifer Deslauriers
Robert Eisner
Elaine Feingold

Sharon Feingold
Beth Finn
Marlene Pollock & Dan Gilbarg
Diane Gilbert
Laurie Glasser
Sam Giammalvo's Auto Sales
L. Michael Gouveia, DMD
Robin & Richard Gross
Robert N. Gurnitz
Heather Haggerty
Kelly Haggerty
Marilyn Halter
Sandra Imbriani
Marilyn & Howard Kass
Jeffrey Katz
John Landry
Karen Larson
Judy Lebolt
Brent & Holly Lestage

Pamela Marean
Rachel Maslow
Susan & Larry Myerson
Victor & Shirley Palestine
Jeannette Ramirez
Janna Renzi
Thomas Rood
Jim & Kerry Rose
Jaclyn Rubin
Melinda Rubin
Donna & Thomas Sargent, Sr.
The Sarner Family
Wendy Squitieri & Dan Scatorchio
Ronald & Ada Jill Schneider
Ed Siegal
Judith & Robert Sterns
Rand & Dale Torman
Anne & Jerry Whitney
Barry S. Yarchin

Contents

FOREWORD

I first met Abe Landau in the mid-1960s as a teenager working behind the counter in my parents' store. The short gentleman with thick arms and strawberry hair came in to purchase thread, buttons and other notions. My mother knew him well.

"This is Mr. Landau, the tailor. He has a shop downtown." Hello, Mr. Landau. A bit of silence. "Do you see the number on Mr. Landau's forearm?" My mother wasn't afraid to broach this subject. She knew him quite well, having had occasion to chat with him at length, as she did with many of her customers.

"Mr. Landau is a Holocaust survivor. The tattoo is the number they gave him in the concentration camp." Abe stood there, sizing me up, evaluating my reaction. He wore a sly, smirky, half-smile on his face, not cocky, but one of confidence, certitude, pride. He said nothing.

Finally, I muttered in a ridiculous teenage way, "Wow, that must have been incredible." "Yes," he chuckled, "Why don't you come to my shop sometime and I'll tell you about it." That sounded fine, but not likely.

I did finally make it to the tailor shop—for my own reasons. I had caught the upper sleeve of my new leather jacket on a nail, enough to make a slight tear. Damn. Something had to be done. Well, perhaps Abe the Tailor could fix it. So after school one day I went down to the tailor shop on Pleasant Street. From the narrow portico on the street, the door opened into an even narrower staircase. Small hand-made signs directed me straight up the stairs to the door on the left. I walked in, and there he was, his glasses balanced on the tip of his nose. He was fiddling, working, fussing with some garment.

A kind-looking lady was sitting in a chair farther back, in the corner near the window. It was his wife, Freida. "Mr. Landau, do you remember me? I'm the…"

"Yes. I know who you are. What can I do for you?" His tone was friendly.

"Well, I tore my jacket and I'd like to know if there's any way you can fix it."

"Let me see it. Yes. Leave it here and come back in a couple of days." The lady smiled. She was sewing something by hand and never broke stride.

Fine. Thank you.

I never thought to ask about his tattoo. In those days, we didn't learn much about the Holocaust in school. At least not in parochial school. Were it not for the remarkable performance of Rod Steiger in "The Pawnbroker" and the driving narrative of Laurence Olivier in "World at War" (which I loved), I might know nothing of this momentous event. When I returned to pick up my jacket two days later, I marveled at the seamless repair he had made with what looked like iron-on bonding tape. That simple. Okay, what's the cost? "No charge," and he flashed a smile that warmed the soul. I glanced at Freida, who was also smiling.

Well, thank you very much, Mr. Landau.

I didn't fully understand why there was no charge. It wasn't an expensive job, for sure. It was Abe saying thank you to my parents through me for their friendliness to him. They understood each other. Second generation Americans from the Middle East, my folks understood the immigrant struggle, the scowls of strangers, the haunting whispers that you don't belong.

Some years later—one sunny spring afternoon in 1993—while stationed in my small basement office in a vintage cape-style home on Mechanics Lane, I noticed an elderly gentleman shuffling near my doorway, peering inside as he fiddled with the handle, trying to open the door into my hobbit hole. It was the diminutive Abe Landau carrying a large box. Inside was a four hundred-page manuscript that he cradled like a precious Ming vase. "Mr. Thomas, I have here my story of the Holocaust. Do you think you want to publish it?"

Now, I do like people who are direct and to the point, but Abe caught me almost speechless. Of course I wanted to publish his book. But could I? Could Spinner do justice to this remarkable story? Could we research it properly and market it nationally? Well, maybe. We talked for some time about the possibilities. Clearly, Abe wasn't going to accept something less than what he envisioned. After all, Holocaust memoirs and oral history were documentary du jour. Spielberg had just finished *Schindler's List*, and the Shoah Foundation had already contacted Abe about taping an interview.

Abe left the manuscript and went on his way. I read it and knew immediately that we should publish it, but I didn't know when. We would need to put a team of editors together and raise some funds. Besides, our plate was full, so I put it aside, as I do with most everything, and returned to the projects at hand.

Abe and I would meet several more times. We talked of a plan to publish his book, but mostly we argued world politics—Israel, Palestine, Lebanon, the Soviet Union. He loved world history and politics and, like myself, he loved to argue. He was a great communicator, attuned to every nuance of speech, facial expression and body language. There was no hedging with this man. He believed we would publish his book and he didn't like waiting. He was very confident.

Well, like growing old—which comes fast and seems to increase exponentially with every passing day—the manuscript slipped into semi-retirement, not to be consulted or mentioned for several years. Abe turned his attention toward building the Holocaust Memorial, and was soon engaged in public speaking and lecturing at schools throughout the region. His prominence in the community grew daily. Spinner Publications, too, was growing. We moved into new digs on William Street and became a part of the fabric of the city. With an expanded staff and renewed energy, we revisited the project and began putting a team together. Then, suddenly, in 1998 Abe was incapacitated by a massive stroke.

When Abe passed in January 2000, I thought it might mean the end of plans. That is, until the day Eddie Rudnick paid us a visit. Abe's longtime friend and biggest fan, Ed was determined to revive the project and get the book in print. Ed didn't want to just know if we were interested in publishing, he wanted to know what exactly needed to be done to make it happen. Music to my ears.

Ed and I began meeting in late 2001. He understood that money would have to be raised through sponsorships and grants because we had none. He would help. We would find editors and researchers to pull it together. And so we began anew.

Unfortunately, Ed, too, passed suddenly—in 2003. In memoriam, I was determined to finish the job. It was important, not just for Abe and Freida, but for their family, for Ed and everyone else.

So here we are, nearly twelve years after Abe's passing and the relevance of his story is immutable—as it was in 1982 when he was first interviewed, and in 1993 when he brought the manuscript to my door. Some things never change.

Meanwhile, the specter of another holocaust hovers over civilization worldwide. Human beings seem bent on annihilating one another as horrific atrocities take place on every continent. Increasingly, violence and terror are inflicted on people because of their ethnicity or religion. A culture of mistrust surrounds many nations and communities. This was true in 1982, and it's true today.

At the dawn of the last days of the "Greatest Generation," it becomes all the more important to learn whatever lessons we can from their experiences. Holocaust survivors are few among us, and unfortunately, Abe is no longer here to teach the children or give us counsel. Thankfully, he leaves this record of his life, momentary yet far-reaching in its message of faith, tolerance and humankind's never-ending quest for liberty and freedom.

– Joseph D. Thomas, Publisher

Abe's Journey ~ 1922–1950

April 25, 1922   Born in Wilczyn, 50 miles east of Poznań in west central Poland.

1931, Age 9   Moves to Kalisz, Poland, a city of 52,000 with 15,300 Jews.

1933   Moves back to Wilczyn. Goes to private and public schools.

Nov. 11, 1939   German army invades Wilczyn on Polish Independence Day.

March 1940   Jews in Wilczyn rounded up and sent to Zagórów, village of about 2,000.

Aug. 20, 1941   Arrested and sent to ZAL[1] Inowrocław, 52 miles north of Zagórów.

Sept 1941   Marched about 3 miles with 34 boys to ZAL Rąbinek. Makes railroad ties.

Aug. 1942   Sent by rail to ZAL Gutenbrunn (Kobylepole), 70 miles west of Rąbinek.

Feb. 1943   Sent by truck and train to ZAL Gleiwitz to work in coal mines.

Aug. 1943   Sent by train and truck to KZ[2] Auschwitz Birkenau.

Feb. 1944   Sent by train to KZ Dachau.

April 1944   Sent by train to KZ Buchenwald concentration camp.

May 1944   Sent by train to ZAL Łagisza (Auschwitz subcamp).

June 1944   Sent on kitchen duty to ZAL Będzin during internment at Łagisza.

July 1944   Sent by train to KZ Buna Monowitz (Auschwitz III).

Jan. 19, 1945   Auschwitz evacuated; Abe sent on "death march" to Gleiwitz.

Jan. 1945   Sent by train to KZ Dora.

Feb. 1945   Trucked to KZ Ellrich.

March 1945   Put on "death train" through Poland, Czechoslovakia, Austria and Germany.

April 1945   Arrives at KZ Bergen-Belsen, which has just been liberated.

Late Fall 1945   Gets apartment in Hannover.

Sept. 1946   Marries Freida in Bergen-Belsen; makes home in Hannover.

Feb. 2, 1950   Emigrates to the United States; arrives with Freida in New Bedford.

1. ZAL: Zwangsarbeitslager / Forced Labor Camp.
2. KZ: Konzentrationslager / Concentration Camp. This abbreviation was used by the prison population and adopted by officials because it has a sharper sound than the official Nazi abbreviation, KL.

EAST PRUSSIA

Inowroclaw & Rabinek

Gutenbrunn

Wilczyn

Zagórów

Warsaw

POLAND

Gleiwitz

Lagisza & Będzin

Birkenau

Buna / Monowitz

Auschwitz Camps

Death March
January 1945

CZECHOSLOVAKIA

Vienna

HUNGARY

ROM

Abe Landau looks from his tailor shop window onto Pleasant Street, New Bedford, 1962.

– Milton Silvia photograph, Spinner Archives

Introduction

My Obligation to Speak

My left forearm bears the number 141282—an unbroken reminder of the thirteen Nazi labor and concentration camps I survived. The number identifies me as loudly as if it were stamped across my forehead. And it burns an agony into my soul that I cannot describe. In the night, without sleep, I relive the nightmare of those horrible years. I wish I could extinguish the pain and memories, but then I realize I must not. It is my obligation to remember.

For decades I kept the Holocaust locked up inside of me. I felt ashamed to have survived. Surely, I thought, people would not want to hear of such horrors. However, I cannot bear to hear denials that the Holocaust took place, negating the suffering of millions. Such denials nullify the murder of my entire extended family and stoke the lies that feed the flames of bigotry and hatred. So I must speak.

The story of the Final Solution, the plight of the Jewish people of Europe during World War II, entails a level of atrocity that transcends the horrors of ordinary war and involves more than the impetus to kill. Many corporations profited from the slaughter. Companies built ovens and supplied gas for extermination. Pharmaceutical firms tested drugs on camp inmates. Human beings were reduced to consumable raw materials, even recycled into the Nazi war economy. I worked in Force Labor Command 167, two miles from Auschwitz, where I. G. Farben, a sprawling corporation, developed deadly chemicals and experimented with poison gases such as Zyklon B, which could kill two thousand people in less than thirty minutes at a cost of half a cent each.[1]

In some cases, the trains that carried Jews to the death camps also carried German civilians in comfortable passenger cars. As they traveled for business and pleasure, some would pass through the city of Oświęcim (Auschwitz). The railroad station was only a mile from the death houses. The stench of burning bodies spread throughout the area. When the American army liberated Dachau, the ovens were still warm and lined with human ashes. Local residents complained about the stench, not about the slaughter. Yet when it was over, these same people said they did not know.

Many who staffed and operated the machinery of genocide were not black-booted soldiers or monsters such as Eichmann, Goring, and Goebbels. There were thousands of ordinary people who helped in one way or another or whose cooperation made the Holocaust a reality. People had mouths but did not speak, eyes but did not see.

I saw it all. I saw the red flames from the crematorium reach high into the sky. I saw many thousands of people—Jews and others—priests, rabbis, nuns, fathers and mothers, sons and daughters, children, the sick and the mentally ill—waiting to be processed and burned in the crematorium. The ghosts of the victims rise from their graves and tug at our conscience. Human skeletons in striped uniforms, with hollow eyes, implore us to recall the crimes committed against them.

I am one of the fortunate ones. I survived Hitler's "Final Solution," but my travelogue is a sojourn through hell. I was seventeen when I was driven from our home and denied my youth, my religion and eventually my entire family. Imprisoned in thirteen different labor and concentration camps, shaved from head to toe, dressed in a zebra suit, I worked long hours at hard labor, eating only bread and watered-down soup, sleeping in bunks with dirty straw, lice and vermin. Many times I came close to being hanged, shot or experimented on. As the war neared its end, we were shipped in cattle cars, back and forth across Poland, Czechoslovakia, Austria and Germany. I survived the death march from Auschwitz to Gleiwitz and a death train from Ellrich to Bergen-Belsen.

Most Americans do not believe genocide could happen here with our long tradition of freedom and democracy. With this, sadly I disagree. I believe the possibility of genocide exists in all populations, for the potential is rooted in human nature.

The Holocaust must not be forgotten, not just for the sake of the Jews, but for all of humanity. If civilization is to survive, mankind must learn to recognize evil when it first appears and halt it before it spreads like the Nazi epidemic. We must speak up and teach in our synagogues, churches, mosques and schools and insist that the world not forget or deny what was done.

I say to all, let the recollection of the Holocaust ignite respect, love and understanding in our souls for every human being, regardless of race, religion, or nationality.

Abe is heartbroken when he finds this racist warning pasted beneath the cheerful clipping on the inside door to his tailor shop, 1972.

Ron Rolo / Standard-Times photograph, Spinner Archives

At age six, Abe and his cheder school classmates pose with their rabbi. Abe is fourth from left. – Landau Family Collection

Chapter I

Life in Wilczyn

In my darkest days, memory kept me alive. I could go back in my mind and remember things—my mother kneading bread dough at the kitchen table, my father sewing in his workshop, purple wildflowers blowing in my grandfather's fields. My life then was so ordinary and so fine.

I grew up in a country town named Wilczyn, in west central Poland. I was born in 1922—although I would later have to change my birth date on many occasions, sometimes making myself younger, sometimes older, in order to save my life. In my early memories, everything was good. We were blessed with vast fields and farms surrounding our home, land owned by my paternal grandparents. My grandfather was a wealthy wheat dealer, a speculator who bought hundreds of acres of wheat and corn even before the fields were seeded. He was a risk-taker and usually came out ahead.

For the most part, we were better off than our neighbors. Besides our large garden, we owned chickens, geese and a horse, thanks to my father, who made good money as a custom clothes designer. He didn't just repair clothes for the average person; he designed and made custom clothes for the Polish intelligentsia—barons and princes. A clever man, my father also had business dealings with wealthy Germans and built a strong network of friends. Sometimes I delivered packages to them on my bike. If they lived on a farm or an estate, I often came back with the gift of a chicken or cherries or potatoes.

Life in rural Poland was still very feudalistic. Throughout the countryside, barons and princes lived on large estates or plantations and had thousands of Polish peasants working the land. One day I was looking out the window and saw a *ksiaze* (prince) coming right to our house to do business with my father. What a sight! I ran outside and joined the neighbors who had gathered in the street. There, right in front of our eyes, was a team of eight beautifully dressed horses, a coach adorned in regalia and a noble coachman at the reins. The prince emerged, so obese he could hardly walk. It didn't matter. Everyone present, especially the elders, and even those looking on from a distance, bent down and kneeled. The closest ones kissed his hand. This was the custom.

When I was still quite young, we moved for a time to the city of Kalisz, about 25 miles north. My father already had many customers there, and the larger population offered him more opportunity. The city had about 100,000 people with a large Jewish population, which made us feel at home. I liked Kalisz because it was my mother's hometown, and my maternal grandparents still lived there. My grandfather worked very hard in his bakery so that his children could be well educated. We moved in with them.

My mother was well liked in town. People knew her, not just because she grew up there, but also because she was a midwife and served everyone who needed her in a kind way. When we walked around town, people recognized her, and that made me proud. She often traveled outside of Kalisz, going from place to place, and she never encountered any prejudice. I liked it best, though, when I didn't have to share her with anybody, especially my two younger sisters and brother.

When we were alone, she often told me stories of her youth. One particular story haunted her—and me. During the War for Independence in 1918, the Poles were trying to beat back the Germans and Russians, who were occupying the city. She often heard fighting on nearby streets—there was no escaping it. One night she was reclining on her bed, listening to heavy fighting and it seemed closer than usual. Her windows were open, her curtains drawn, and she thought she was safe. Exhausted, she fell asleep, only to be awakened by the splintering crash of a bullet that pierced the headboard just inches above her head. I'd often ask her how she could sleep under those conditions, and she would tell me that she was not afraid. But she told me the story many times, in an effort to expel her lingering fears, I suspect.

We were close to both sets of grandparents, as well as our uncles. My mother's three brothers played a big part in my life. One was a clothes designer, another a lawyer; the third was an important businessman, and a very religious one at that. This uncle paid special attention to me and took me places I might not have gone. He was a *ba'al koreh*[1] at the synagogue, a specialist in reading the Torah. When we were in Kalisz, he would take my hand as we walked to the synagogue, a dark and conservative place, and he encouraged me to listen as he read. I fell in love with the melody of the Torah, and it became a lifelong love affair.

View of Market Square in Kalisz on Poland Independence Day, circa 1930.

Polish National Digital Archives

In the large cities of Europe, the Ashkenazi Jews[2] went to conservative synagogues, and my uncle introduced me to this world. The men looked a little foreign to my young eyes, all dressed in black, but I was enchanted as I watched the rabbi, the cantor, and the ba'al koreh perform the service. I loved the ceremony. Even though I was a child and had no formal musical training, I knew I had the inner strength and passion to one day sing. Sometimes I felt I could sing before all the world. Surprisingly, my mother's family was mostly secular (except for this particular uncle), but we all loved the services. We loved the ritual and ceremony and song. I think I loved it most of all.

Eventually we moved back to Wilczyn and my father's family. I remember moving back and forth, between country and city, and I loved both places, the peace of the country and the excitement of the city. My father's family was orthodox, and two of his brothers were rabbis. Herzl Landau, from Kolo, was among the most famous cantors in Europe. I'm proud of the Landau name, as it belonged to intellectuals from generations back. Though the Landau family had been in Poland since the time of my great-grandfathers, my father told me that we originally came from Germany. When I became old enough to investigate the Landau family roots, my father would say, "I'll tell you more when you're older." Unfortunately, we would not get much older together.

As I grew up, my paternal grandfather filled me with stories. One of his favorites was the story of the Russian gold medal that he kept in his room, which he felt greatly honored to have earned. We had this ritual we played out whenever I came upon the medal. "Zaideh," I'd ask, "who gave you this medal?" And he'd answer proudly, "Tsar Nicholas II."

He told me that he'd won the medal for bravery as a Russian officer in the Russo-Turkish War of 1878. But things didn't go well for him after his heroic moment. When he lived on the

The Great Synagogue in Kalisz contained valuable artifacts and was plundered by the Nazis at the time of this photo in 1940. To add to their humiliation, the congregants were forced to take it apart with their own hands. This may be the orthodox synagogue where Abe worshiped with his uncle.

Russian border, for example, he witnessed the persecution and killing of many Jews. As he recalled these Russian pogroms, especially in the smaller cities, he shook his head at such cruelty.

It seemed odd that he was so proud of his Russian gold medal when, not long after, the Russians were beating up on the Jews. In his mind, the medal was not tarnished; it was earned honorably.

I was lucky to get a public education and a good Jewish education, too. I went to public school until mid-afternoon, then attended *cheder*, a Jewish school, and sometimes studied until 8 PM. I began the Jewish school when I was six and planned to continue through age twelve. Between the two schools, I got an interesting education: Yiddish and Hebrew, Bible stories like Sodom and Gomorrah, and the history of Jewish culture. We spoke Yiddish at home, though family members knew Polish, too. In the smaller cities, Jews generally spoke Yiddish and in the larger cities, they spoke Polish.

It would take an hour to get dressed for cheder. First I would put on the tefillin, a leather holder attached to my arm and neck by small straps—my father wouldn't let me leave the house without it. It contained important chapters from the Torah written on four pieces of parchment. I also wore a *yarmulke*[3] on my head. Most of the time, I liked school, but not always. The teachers and rabbis were strict, and when we were bad, they slapped us on the rear or head. Sometimes, if we were very bad, we were put beneath a trapdoor in the floor, where only the thinnest streams of light sifted into the blackness. We could stay there for half an hour, feeling lonely and shamed, a frightening experience for a child. I tried to be good and studied hard so this wouldn't happen.

I began attending public school around age five; we wore blazers and slacks and were usually well-behaved. But I was sometimes punished for various misdeeds, such as being late to class or showing a lack of respect, although I obeyed the rules most of the time. In Poland, teachers were revered far more than government officials. Any time you passed by a teacher, no matter where you were, you doffed your hat

and bowed your head. The same was true for a policeman, priest or rabbi. Even if he were across the street, you always tipped your hat and bowed. This was the custom.

I was about eleven at this time, and I liked school, but it began feeling less safe than it did before. I had many non-Jewish friends, but something was changing. We thought we were all friends and then, for no reason at all, a Polish classmate would call out, "Jew, go to Palestine." We Jewish kids were becoming afraid of some of the Polish kids who were arrogant and always looking to start fights.

This happened in the city, too. When the Poles got drunk on vodka—and they liked their vodka—they became ornery and looked around for the nearest Jew. One drunken man regularly sat on the steps of my home and shouted obscenities; then, he would go from one Jewish home to another, waving a stick or whip, trying to hurt and scare people.

We didn't stand up to them when they behaved like this—no one said anything. We ignored such behavior and hoped it would go away. Actually, my own family was less harassed than others. Some got stones thrown through their windows and suffered quietly in their homes, trying to make themselves invisible. But I was beginning to see something I hadn't seen before—we were afraid of the Polish people and we lived from one bitter incident to another. Fearful or not, we had to face the reality of every day; the fact was we lived with the Poles. We shared the land, we went to school with them, we did business with them.

Yes, we did business. The Polish people shopped for food at the kosher markets and ate in Jewish restaurants, but they liked their own sausages best. We would peek through the butchers' window and watch them at work, smelling the garlicky fragrance of the kielbasa as it drifted outside. It was very nice. Europeans ate a lot of pork. When someone wanted to insult a Pole, he called him a "Polish pig."

When a scandal broke out in a nearby family, it made a big impression on me and showed me how deep and complex things really were on both the

Jewish and Christian sides. A Jewish neighbor—one of seven brothers—joined the Polish army, and while in the service, met and married a Christian girl. It was a sin for a Jew to marry a Gentile and a really grave sin for this family. His father was a pious Jew and stood out in town with his long beard, wearing a fur hat known as a *shtreimel*.[4] Married Haredi men grew beards and wore such hats on the Sabbath and Jewish holidays. This man became very bitter over his son's marriage and was shunned by other Jews. It put a huge blot on his family for the rest of his life.

The young couple eventually had a son, who went to school with me. Though the boy was well aware his father was Jewish, he was very bigoted against Jews. I couldn't understand it. He harassed me continually and swore at me in Polish, "Fucking Jew, go to Palestine." He was so full of self-loathing and hate. I believe he felt tormented about his family situation, and so he tormented others. Eventually he and his father grew distant from his brothers, who were all practicing Jews, and they moved away.

I was also seeing other things at school that I hadn't noticed before, or didn't think much about. In the sixth grade, we were together as a class, Jews and Gentiles, but not really. During the day we had a religious hour where the priests came in and taught Catholicism, and the Jewish children left for recess. But during this hour, the priests were teaching bigotry and hatred, though they may not have realized it. The priests would say, "Jid, you killed Jesus," and "you used the blood of our martyrs in Passover," and other nonsense. The teachers knew what the priests were teaching and sometimes brought it up in class, expressing their own anti-Semitism. You could feel this sentiment by the way you were treated. Nearly every day I would leave school feeling accused.

As I grew older, I listened and observed more than before. This growing estrangement between Christian and Jew was showing up in small ways and large. I used to go out with some of the teens from the Christian neighborhoods, and we'd get together for special occasions like sporting events or concerts. This didn't happen anymore. Jews

Abe Landau at age 16 with his public school mates and teachers in Wilczyn, 1938. Abe is in the second-to-last row, second from right.

were beginning to keep more to themselves. We thought we would be safer this way.

There were happier images from those days that remain with me. I loved to go fishing. My grandfather owned property on a lake in Wilczyn, and every Friday morning my mother and I would get up at four, before sunrise, to make preparations for my fishing trip. Because Friday was Shabbos, my mother prepared the food by hand on Thursday night. She made a lunch of gefilte fish, and in the morning, would pack pre-baked breads and cakes for me to bring to the bakery before the journey. Since Wilczyn had just one Jewish bakery, everyone in the city brought their pre-baked goods there.

So I would set out, pole and lunch in hand, on a three- or four-mile hike through dense forests to the lake—the birds singing beautifully and the sun streaming down through the trees. Occasionally, when I was near a village, I'd see people passing by on foot and peasants walking along pathways on their way to work. It was serene, a beautiful scene. I think of Wilczyn, my birthplace, my first home, and recall this scene. It stayed alive inside me while all around me fell to ruin.

Trouble in the Markets (1938-1939)

I liked the ongoing street life in Wilczyn, which was always colorful and lively, and market day was the best. On Tuesdays and Fridays, we had open markets in the town square, where just about everything was for sale—clothing, cheese, meats, vegetables and even furniture. The vendors arrived from surrounding cities and towns the night before to mark the spot where they would set up their tables, and everyone fought for a decent place on the square. Soon thousands of people arrived to buy their supplies, and you could hear a vibrant chorus of voices rise and fall with all the mingling, deal-making and selling. It seemed to me that most of the traders were Jewish and very poor, but it didn't matter— market day was marvelous, like a carnival.

Then, one day, something went wrong. We heard shouting and saw fights breaking out in the crowd. At first, we were confused. What was going on? Soon a cadre of Polish thugs arrived in the square, mostly older boys, and began beating up the Jewish merchants with their fists. Having cowed the merchants, they took out their knives and sliced the tents from the rear, stealing

The tranquil Lake Wilczynski, 2011. Here, Abe went fishing near his grandfather's property.

Dariusz Goiński

26

Open market in the Jewish quarter of Warsaw, 1930s.
- Yad Vashem Archives, courtesy of Ruth Burns

Clothing merchants at the marketplace in Szczercow, Poland, 1939.
– United States Holocaust Memorial Museum

all the goods they could get their hands on. A disaster for the vendors who had come from great distances, by horse and wagon, in snow and rain, and then waited all night in hopes of making a small profit the next day! The attack terrified them.

At that moment, I understood like never before why it was not easy to be a Jew in Poland—we lived in muted terror all the time, never quite sure what would happen to us. We knew in our bones we were not welcome here, though this was our homeland, too. My parents and neighbors had experienced such events

before, sudden, unexpected acts of terror against the Jews, but this was my first time, and it was chilling. I could not stop thinking about what I had seen. I realized this was just the beginning of my education. And I had learned a new word—pogrom.[5]

Spring turned into summer and summer made me hopeful again. I was out of school and eager for adventure when opportunity appeared. My uncle owned a store where he sold dry goods and ready-to-wear apparel. Since not enough buyers lived in the area, he traveled twice a month to sell his goods in the outlying areas. His

Horse-drawn carts line up on the outskirts of a crowded outdoor market in Oświęcim, Poland (later Auschwitz) before the war, 1939.

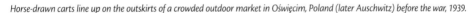

United States Holocaust Memorial Museum, courtesy of Hilda Tayar

family usually helped, but his son had gone off to the army and his daughter was not feeling well these days. He asked my parents if I could go with him as his helper. He said to me, "Why don't you come with us, just for the relaxation. Come and see how we sell the goods, and you can help watch people who come in." My parents agreed.

I was excited that evening as we loaded his merchandise into the wagon, filling it with suit stands and display items as well as goods. Exhausted, we retired early and rose at three in the morning to begin our journey.

It was still dark as we traveled by horse and wagon to Mogilno, a small city about 20 miles north of Wilczyn. It was a pretty city with a large German population. Not many Jews lived here, or in Poznań, the provincial capital, as they did not feel safe. Both cities were known to be terribly anti-Semitic. The Jews who settled here were wealthy families who built their own beautiful synagogues and kept to themselves.

The sun came out and promised us a beautiful day. As we entered the town, we could hear the bustling marketplace with hundreds of merchants arranging their goods. It was all so colorful, I thought, as I scanned the bright tables and wares. At first, our own little business was thriving. Everything was peaceful and busy, and I loved being in the midst of all the activity. My job was to look out for shoplifters, and that is what I did. But things changed quickly. I heard a bang, followed by a bang, bang. The noise was so loud I nearly jumped out of my skin, thinking a bomb had gone off nearby.

In the distance, I saw a small truck flying down the road heading toward the market, looking like it was going to mow us down, but as it got nearer, a bunch of tough guys jumped out. I will never forget this—they started terrorizing people, plowing through the entire length of tents where the goods were set up. In the ensuing madness, vendors were scrambling to take down their displays, people were crying, goods were stolen, everybody was moving, running, hiding. So this was how our day ended, in chaos and tears.

We just wanted to get out of there and go home. On the road back, my uncle looked like a beaten man. "Oh, Lord," he moaned, "today we should have come home with a profit and instead our money and merchandise are gone."

Our pleasant day had turned into a disaster.

Contemporary view along Konin Street in Wilczyn, the main street leading to the old central square, 2011. The old synagogue faced Konin Street, and many Jewish homes surrounded it, including Abe's.

Jarosław Buziak

Wilczyn and Kalisz

Before the Nazi invasion, the towns of Kalisz and Wilczyn were home to thriving Jewish communities. In Kalisz, one of the oldest Jewish communities in Poland, about 15,000 Jews lived among the population of about 90,000. The community was located mainly in the northwestern portion of the city and was home to a variety of shops, cafes, and artisans, as well as a grand synagogue and Jewish school.

[United States Holocaust Memorial Museum]

A 1939 census shows Wilczyn as a small agricultural community with 72 homes and 630 residents, including 147 Jews. While the Jews and Poles lived in relative harmony in Wilczyn, such was not the case in Kalisz. In 1937, amid an atmosphere of anti-Semitism, fueled by an anti-Jewish newspaper, Kalisz gentiles imposed a boycott on Jewish shops, forcing Jewish merchants to relocate to a certain area of the marketplace. A culture of violence festered as pogroms took place on Jewish residents traveling isolated roads. These occurrences increased following the Nazi invasion until there was virtually no Jewish culture remaining.

A Jewish family strolls along a street in Kalisz, Poland, 1935.
– United States Holocaust Memorial Museum

Funeral procession in Wilczyn town square, ca. 1920.
– United States Holocaust Memorial Museum

Map of Wilczyn, 1940.

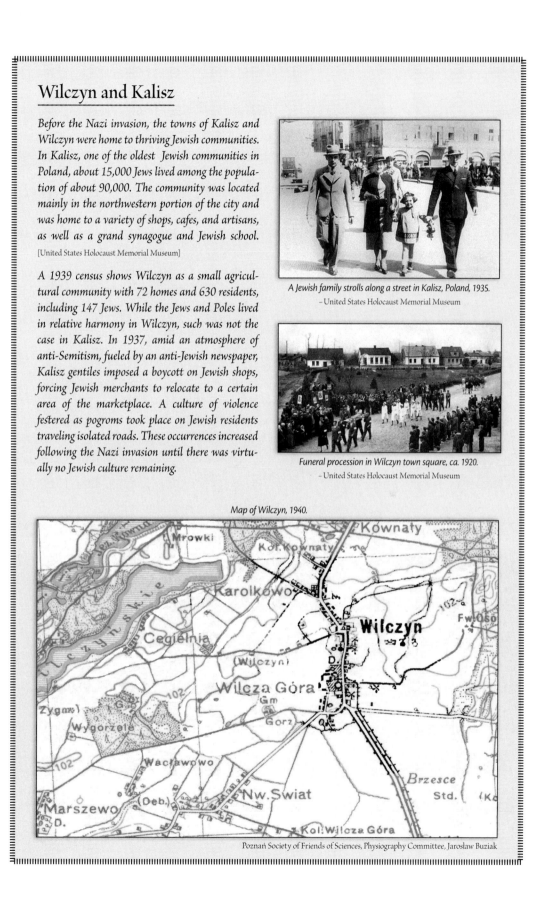

Poznań Society of Friends of Sciences, Physiography Committee, Jarosław Buziak

29

Crowds of Volksdeutche line the streets of Poznań to greet the conquering Germans as liberators, September 1939.

– Heinz Fremke, German Federal Archives

CHAPTER II

THE INVASION OF POLAND

Looking back now, I believe the Jews in Poland were living in darkness. There were very few newspapers and hardly anyone had a radio, so there was very little news coming in from the outside world. And, yes, we were naïve about what could happen to Poland. After all, my father had many German customers around Wilczyn for whom he made expensive clothing, and he was very friendly with them. I often visited families with him and sometimes I rode my bike out to a farm or estate to deliver their merchandise. We knew about Hitler's invasion of Czechoslovakia in 1938, but we never imagined it could happen here. Even with the evidence—anti-Semitism all around us, increasing numbers of pogroms, rumors that the Germans were having secret meetings and, most important, that Hitler was preparing for war, even with all that, we did not believe war would come to us. Rumors, after all, are rumors, and what does anybody really know? At most, we believed that war might break out, go on for three or four months and quickly end. We still believed that the *Volksdeutsche*[1], in cahoots with the Polish hooligans, were more dangerous than Hitler—until September 1939, when Hitler invaded Poland.

My father traveled frequently as a textile designer and on the day of the invasion, he was away on business in the industrial city of Łódź. At 5 AM we were awakened by the sound of planes flying overhead, rattling our houses. We ran to the street to join the crowds and heard talk that the Germans were fighting in Danzig (now Gdansk) in northern Poland. My father hadn't yet returned home and we were frantic. When he finally arrived, we were all over him in gratitude, and he informed us that the Polish army was fighting the Germans in northern Poland. All night long we watched as Polish troops marched through Wilczyn on their way north, and we wondered in particular about the whereabouts of my cousin, David Bloom, who was a highly educated lawyer and a two-star major in the army. Although many Jews were in the army, it was unusual for a Jew to have such a high military rank. David was a close friend of Marshall Pilsudski, a former Polish dictator.

When David finally returned to Wilczyn, he told us stories of the fighting, and we were grateful to finally get some real news, grim as it was. He was with members of the Polish artillery who had engaged in fierce fighting in Kutno, not far from Warsaw. He said that thousands of horses belonging to the Polish army died in the line of fire, and it was a terrible sight. The army was brave and killed great numbers of Germans in the beginning of the war but finally surrendered because it had nothing left to fight with.

The German occupation prompted entire families to migrate from big to smaller cities like Wilczyn, where they thought they would be safer. In the first few months of the occupation, we grew more pessimistic about the fate of the Jewish people. My father's two brothers and their families left Będzin and Kolo to move in with us for the next couple of months. They were stricken with fear, and one cousin immediately fled to Russia. Soon another cousin, an accomplished opera singer, took his entire family to Russia. We never heard from them again. Two uncles on my mother's side had also fled to

Russia and ended up living in a ghetto after the war. But that was the last I heard of any of them.

On November 11, 1939, my family and I were working around the house, too busy with our chores to look up and notice something unusual happening nearby. The war still seemed like it was somewhere else, even with the occupation of nearby cities. The General had fled, and we knew something was happening to the Jews in Germany. But on this day the war came home when a German column of tanks, jeeps and artillery roared through the streets of Wilczyn. The people looked out their windows and followed the ominous procession with fearful eyes, in complete silence.

We knew very well what this occupation meant, but we weren't sure what would happen next. It remained eerily quiet for the next few days while soldiers patrolled the town on foot. Most obvious were the SS guards dressed in black uniforms, and storm troopers dressed in green. There were also swarms of *Hitlerjugend* (Hitler Youth),[2] looking like Boy Scouts in service to the devil.

Hitler Youth march from the newly renamed Wilhelmsplatz in Poznań to the inauguration of Governor Greiser at the castle, November 1939.

The weather matched our moods, dark and gloomy, while the Germans scoured the city looking for Jews to put to work. Like a cattle roundup, they went from house to house gathering Jews.[3] Friends, neighbors and acquaintances were summoned and put to work. One evening my mother was in bed nursing her nervous stomach, and I heard a loud knock on the door. I was afraid to answer and afraid not to, so I opened it slowly, shyly like a little kid. This big man stood in the hallway, a German SS officer,[4] and his size and hard face nearly frightened me to death. He said, *Verfluchte Juden.* You goddamn Jews. We need five boys to go to work." Too terrified to speak, I followed him out in the dark. A small Polish boy, about ten, was waiting for him outside and gave him instructions. The boy said, "In this house is a Jew." The boy led him to five different houses and I followed along as he yanked Jewish boys from each of the houses. They were friends of mine, some as old as twenty. I was the youngest at seventeen.

In small towns like Wilczyn, every Pole knows where the Jews live.[5] The boy was an innocent and knew nothing of what the Germans had planned for us, but he betrayed us, perhaps out of fear for himself. The SS men ordered us into a horse-drawn cart, and we rode three miles outside the city to where German soldiers occupied a lavish villa owned by a Polish prince. Here we were ordered to work, and work we did. We scrubbed boots, packed ammunition, cut wood and prepared their fires; we cleaned the military cars and unloaded trucks; we did whatever we were told. We worked from 6 AM until late at night. Day after day, we were hungry, separated from our families and fearful that we would never see them again. We could not protest any of this if we wanted to stay alive.

One moonlit night, with stars bright in the sky, we finished our work very late, around midnight, and we were more than ready to go home. Instead, the soldiers decided to have some fun with us. They demanded that we unhitch the wagon and fill it with stones. So we loaded the wagon with hundreds of stones; then, we were forced to push the wagon and gallop like

horses along the highway back to Wilczyn. As we pushed, the soldiers fired their guns over our heads to frighten us. This was the first of many times we would feel such Nazi degradation.

The German occupiers relied on the local people to serve their needs. When they needed a skilled tailor, they called on my father, and he catered to them without complaint, repairing and pressing their uniforms. He did what he had to do to survive another day without trouble.

One particular day still plays over in my mind like a bad movie; it became a warning about what was to come. My father had a German friend, a good customer, whose clothes he fit and tailored. They had an easy relationship and always shared a few laughs. On this day, the customer and another man arrived on horseback at our house, unexpectedly, and they offered no greeting. Without saying a word, my father's friend strode into the house, took off his hat and coat and exposed a swastika on his arm. He said to my father, "Look Jacob, we have been friends for so many years. You and I both know what is happening here, and I don't think we can be friends any longer." His voice kept getting louder. "Give us all the material you have in stock."

My father went into shock—he was about to lose his livelihood. The two men proceeded to rob my father of all his fabric and tools. They were without mercy.

His former friend made one last demand. "I don't want to have to drive back and forth. I want your son to load up the wagon and take everything back to my farm." I looked at my father, then at the floor. My father nodded. Shivering with fear, I loaded the wagon with my father's things and drove the team to the man's large farm located in the village. It was already dark as I began unloading. When I finished, he called me into his room and said in German, "You are very lucky. If you had refused to come out tonight, I would have had to kill you."

I felt sick but tried to be polite. "You have been friendly with my father for many years. I never expected this to happen." I remember his reply clearly. His words would ring in my brain for years to come. "The world is different now."

My father's friend was one of the Volksdeutsche and had been involved with the Nationalists behind the scenes for a long time. And they were the people who had made it easy for the Germans to occupy Poland. Though officially Polish citizens, they remained loyal to Germany. And when the invasion and occupation took place, they already knew what was going on; they had laid the groundwork. They were also the ringleaders behind many of the pogroms. Scattered in many different communities, they met in secrecy and were careful not to reveal themselves. But after the invasion, they became a visible part of the occupation by helping to plunder Jewish businesses and looting local stores. We never knew what business would be shut down, who would be killed, who would be the next victim of some insane act. We were overcome with fear.

The Germans were inventive in tormenting us. They forced us to carry out acts of desecration against our Christian neighbors so they would turn against us. The Christians worshiped in chapels situated in the town squares. We could see small crucifixes glowing inside, circling and protecting a statue of the Madonna. Such a chapel sat in the middle of Wilczyn, where Christians went to worship and pray to the Madonna for miracles. If a Jew entered this sacred place and defaced the Madonna, it would be a crime. And we would never do such a thing.

On a cold snowy day in mid-January, German soldiers were marching door to door, rounding up Jewish boys and men. I was among the recruits yet again, and I wondered what plans they had for us tonight. They ordered us to enter the chapel, remove the Madonna and roll her around the city square. We were horrified but went ahead and rolled and flipped and spun her around the square. We thought we would die of cold and exhaustion. Finally, they demanded that we take the Madonna to the beautiful home of one of the wealthiest Jews in Wilczyn and throw it through his front window. We felt such shame and humiliation when we returned home.

The next day a Jewish friend told me the story of what happened after that. A German soldier went to the man's house and said, "Look, we hear you are hiding something in here." The man stood frozen, not knowing what to say. They searched his house and found the Madonna, then demanded the family bury it in the Jewish cemetery. The Poles observed all this and were stunned and confused by the incident. They knew they couldn't blame the Jews.

Another night a sick, elderly man was forced at gunpoint to ride a horse around the city square until he was half dead. Also, Jewish women were regularly ordered to sweep the streets, clean the stairs and do dirty labor. All of this was done to torment and intimidate the Jews. It worked.

The infamous *Krystallnacht*[6] played out in different ways in different cities and towns. In Wilczyn, it happened this way:

It was Friday night and our family was attending the service at the synagogue, which was right across the street from our house. All the other Jewish families were here with us. Suddenly we heard the exploding crash of gunfire nearly blowing out our ears. The blasts

Wehrmacht soldiers go door to door to gather information on Polish civilians, such as this mother and child in Lublin, September 1939.

Falk, German Federal Archives

34

Reichbau Wartheland

The Wartheland was one of four Reichbaue (administrative divisions) created after the invasion of Poland and its annexation to Germany. The Reichbaue were Poznań, Upper Silesia, Danzig, and West Prussia—areas taken from Germany after the Treaty of Versailles. To further establish pre-treaty boundaries for the Third Reich, Hitler also annexed Austria and much of Czechoslovakia before setting his sights on Poland. The province of Poznań was one of the first to be conquered and was renamed Wartheland after the area's major river, the Warta (Warthe in German). This region is the setting of Abe's childhood and the site of his first labor camp. Wilczyn, Kalisz, Inowrocław, and Gutenbrunn were all part of the Reichbau Wartheland.

After annexation, the complete "Germanization" of the Wartheland was underway. The Nazis expelled about a half million Poles and Jews from the area, and resettled about the same number of Germans and Volksdeutsche there. They also renamed many of the cities and towns in German. The culture that the Landau family enjoyed before the war was erased from history. At the end of the war, much of the German population fled the Wartheland. During this flight, some 50,000 perished under harsh weather conditions or were killed by the advancing Red Army. Most of those who survived were later expelled from Poland altogether.

On September 1, 1939, Germany launched a massive, unprovoked "Blitzkrieg" on Poland, deploying over 1.5 million troops, 2,600 tanks, and 2,000 aircraft. Conversely, the Polish military had only 180 tanks and 420 aircraft.

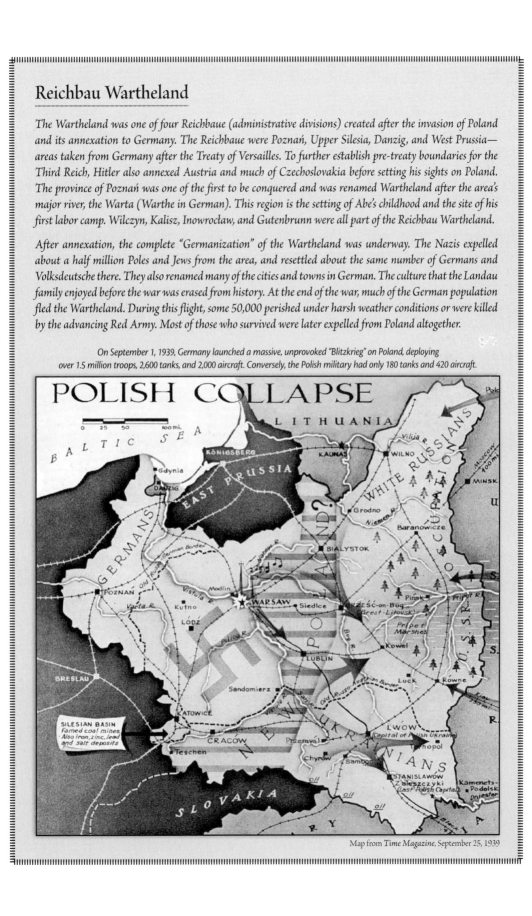

Map from *Time Magazine*, September 25, 1939

35

were coming from every direction, and we tried to pin down the source. "Hey, up there!" someone yelled. We looked up and, dear God, the Germans were shooting in the windows of the synagogue. Fortunately, the windows were high, so the bullets were whizzing over our heads. No one was shot but chaos reigned. Afraid to stay inside, even more afraid to go outside, we huddled where we were for nearly two hours, and when everything became quiet outside we left, hoping we would make it home alive.

In other cities and towns in Poland and Germany, Jewish stores and businesses were looted and burned, people were rounded up, apartments were searched and family treasures were broken. It was all systematically planned and carried out by soldiers. Our situation had become desperate.

Leaving Wilczyn

Living under the German occupation was hell. I grew up in a free country, a free Poland, and suddenly we were hostages in our own land. We had to serve as slaves—providing clothing, cleaning, sewing—living each day in fear, not knowing what would happen.

The Germans had now occupied our city for four months. In the early afternoon on a day in March, 1940, a lightweight artillery truck with six soldiers in the back slowly rolled down our street. One soldier held a loudspeaker and shouted, *"Alle Juden! In einer Stunde werden Sie Ihr Zuhause verlassen müssen...!* All Jews! In one hour you must leave your homes, every Jew must come to the square. One hour. You are allowed to take only what you can carry and nothing more." And just in case we didn't get the message, a group of

soldiers began shooting at the synagogue, flying bullets piercing doors, walls, windows. My father, who was very religious, was well aware that they were destroying the synagogue but he could do nothing. In one hour we had to leave our homes. The older folks were crying in the streets and younger people tried to comfort them.

We had lived in our house for so long, it was unthinkable that we had to leave. Most Jews had treasures from generations back—gold, silver, jewelry—and we had to decide quickly what to take with us. Fortunately, when the occupation began, my father and I took our precious possessions, including my grandmother's diamond ring, and put them in a little wooden box. In a larger box we packed up my father's watches, candelabras and gold chains, all the items he had inherited from my great-great grandmother. We buried the small box in the yard and the larger one under the floorboards. But sadly, we could not bury our house and dig it up when times were better. I was so distraught about leaving our home and neighborhood. I almost wished I could bury myself with the jewelry.

My mother didn't believe we would ever come back. My father, though, was optimistic. "We'll get everything back," he promised. I wonder if he said that to bolster our spirits, especially my mother's. Or maybe he really did believe it. "Maybe you're right," I said, looking into his downtrodden eyes. We buried everything and got ready to go to the square in one hour.

This photograph, entitled "A trek in the district of Poznań, 1940," may well have been Abe's caravan from Wilczyn to Zagórów—a journey through farmland and small towns in west central Poland.

Zeymer, German Federal Archives

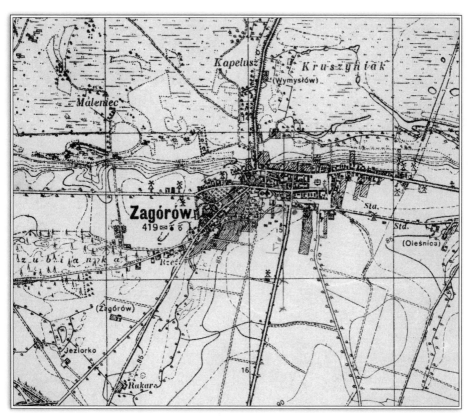

The small city of Zagórów is located about 28 miles south of Wilczyn. Local historian Jaroslaw Buziak gives us this account: "My grandmother told me a story about Jews from Kleczew shtetl near Wilczyn. After having brought Jews from Kleczew to Zagórów, Mayor Diesterheft promised that he would release them from the ghetto if they turned over all their gold and valuables to him. Many Jews accepted his proposal and were given permission to leave the ghetto and walk to their homes in Kleczew, 25 miles away, to retrieve their goods. After the transaction, they were not released from the ghetto." – Poznań Society of Friends of Sciences, Physiography Committee, Jaroslaw Buziak

Chapter III

The Zagórów Ghetto

Our life as refugees had begun. We gathered a few things, packed them in small bundles and walked hurriedly away from our home for the last time. In another small gesture of Nazi contempt, we were told to lock the doors before handing over the keys, as though our stolen life would be safely looked after.

In two hours the square was awash with Jews, drained from dozens of homes across the town. Everyone came, milling and sulking about for several hours—people were crying, some pulling their hair, some going berserk, others just fainting, falling unconscious into the street. It was bedlam. Even the crippled and the infirm were cast away, lying in the street on stretchers. Everyone was confused; no one knew what was happening.

Suddenly, in mid-afternoon, a fleet of what seemed like two hundred horse-drawn wagons[1] driven by Polish farmers came thundering toward the square. In a scene that I would witness many times over, in a manner of orderly chaos, we were forced onto the wagons like sheep on a rail car. Some families became separated; others, like ours, managed to stay together. We were joined by two uncles, a friend and a neighbor—about fifteen or twenty people all packed into the wagon.

My mother was still feeling ill. She had been on medication for a nervous stomach and was often very sick. Lately, my father, too, had been ill. He had diabetes and his condition had worsened by the stress of the occupation and the trauma of leaving our home.

At seventeen, I was the eldest sibling and obliged to give the younger ones strength and hope. My sisters were twelve and ten and my little brother just eight. I looked into their faces and teary eyes and saw sheer terror. My father kept saying, "Don't worry. We're going to be back home in three or four months, maybe five." Did his impassioned faith lead him to believe that this war would really be over in a matter of months? He could never have imagined the savagery that would turn the whole world upside down. No, he would never have believed it.

Thus, my journey began. It would continue five long years.

The wagons traveled in single file in one long
xcolumn, a peculiar sight to the Poles who stood
in the streets of the villages we passed, curiously
watching this endless wagon train go by. After
traveling about thirty miles, across the countryside and through villages, we came to the small
city of Zagórów, which the Germans renamed
Hinterberg in 1939. It was dark when we arrived,
and as we climbed down from the wagons, we
wondered why we had come to such a place. We
stayed in the city square for what seemed like
hours until all the soldiers arrived. From the
square we were taken to homes previously inhab-
ited by Polish families. Some were empty, but
some were still occupied. My family was taken
with three other families and put into a two-
room house. Twenty-two people packed into two
rooms! It was hot and stuffy with so many people
crammed together. No hot water, no electricity,
so we used kerosene lamps or candles. The toilets
were outdoors.

Before this time there were few Jews living
in Zagórów as it was considered such an anti-
Semitic city. But now the Germans had gathered

In Gostynin in Central Poland (part of the new Wartheland), a family
collects its belongings before evacuation. – German Federal Archives

about two thousand of us from cities across the
region—including Wilczyn, Kleczew, Mogilno,
Slesin and Golina—and squeezed us into this
ghetto. We were told we could live here and
stay inside, or go into the city, or work, it didn't
matter. We could mingle, deal, look out for each
other, but we were not to leave the city boundaries. So we learned fairly quickly where the city
ended, and we stayed within it.

Families were given food for a week, maybe
two. In order to get more, we had to go into town

A Jewish family with their life belongings in tow makes their way to an assigned dwelling in the Będzin Ghetto, ca. 1941.

From a Nazi propaganda film, Ghetto Fighters House Archives

and barter with the Polish people. And so we did. At times we fought among ourselves, stealing food from each other in order to eat. The few valuables we brought such as gold coins, rings and heirlooms, we sold to the Polish people. When we had nothing left to trade, we were forced to beg and steal.

By November 1940, we were starving, and my father decided to risk leaving the ghetto to find food. He hired a Polish man with a horse and wagon to take him to the countryside around Wilczyn, where he had Polish friends. I often accompanied him, going door to door, asking for food, and we felt like beggars, stripped of our dignity. We gladly took what they gave us—a few loaves of bread, a few pounds of rice and potatoes.

I will never forget one miserable, cold and rainy day, trudging through the slush and snow on our way back to Zagórów. The worn soles on my shoes flapped with each step, leaving my feet wet and freezing, and I ended up with a dreadful cold. But on this day it was worth it. We brought back enough food to feed the family for a couple of weeks. We were taking a great risk by leaving

Judenviertel!
Den Juden ist das Verlassen dieses Stadtteiles bei Strafe verboten.
Die Ortspolizeibehörde.

Dzielnica żydowska!
Zabrania się Żydom opuszczania tej dzielnicy pod grozbą kary.
Miejscowy Urząd Policyjny.

A sign in both German and Polish, placed at the entrance to the Jewish quarters, reminds Jews that they are forbidden to leave.

Zagórów. We would have been shot if they had caught us. I was terrified, so fearful of the consequences, and one day I told my father I didn't want to do it anymore. He looked at me with great pity and acceptance. For me, it was worse than for him—I didn't have the courage to help my father.

The Germans instituted their own form of ghetto democracy, telling us to appoint a Jewish Council, a group supposedly similar to the Red Cross, though we had no hospitals or schools. It consisted of five or six Jewish policemen, along

A Jewish policeman and a German soldier direct pedestrian traffic across the main street dividing the two parts of the Łódź Ghetto, 1940. The German sign at the entrance to the ghetto reads, "Jewish residential area, entrance is forbidden."

Photograph by Antonii Marianowicz, Jewish Historical Institute, courtesy of Emanuel Ringelblum, United States Holocaust Memorial Museum

with a handful of citizens, whose orders came from a German commandant. As it turned out, the Jewish Council was mainly responsible for recruiting other Jews to work details. If the Germans needed laborers, and they sometimes called for as many as two hundred, then the Jewish Council rounded up the people. If your name was chosen by lottery, a Council member would approach you in the street—"Hey, you need to work today." I usually did road or factory work, which was very hard labor. If you refused to go, you were whipped.

The work we did took us to various locations. One was Slesin, a famous historical city, and a striking one, too. To enter, you walked under a beautiful tall arch, similar to the Arc de Triomphe in France. The inscription on the arch, in Polish, informed us that Napoleon had entered the city with his army. With some amazement, I remembered my grandfather telling me a story about this event.

Napoleon went through Poland en route to Russia in an extremely cold winter. When he arrived in Slesin, he approached a famous rabbi and asked his advice. "I hear you are a very knowledgeable and pious man and I have confidence in you. Can you tell me what is going to happen to me and my army?" The rabbi could not answer right away, but the next day he was out walking and came across a rooster whose comb was completely frozen. He took the rooster to Napoleon and said, "Do you see what happened to the top of the rooster's head? The same thing will happen to you and your army. You will all freeze to death."

One day I had a particularly bad experience with the work detail. I was in a group of about twenty-five boys chosen to do construction on a seven-story building in Golina, and we were expected to live at the site. The job frightened me and so I didn't go. The next day the soldiers came looking for me and ordered my father to accompany me to the police station. They made me bend down over a bench, naked, while one soldier held my legs, the other my arms. My father was ordered to give me sixteen lashes with a leather whip as hard as he could. I screamed as five lengths of leather slashed my back and buttocks

Jewish police, assigned by the Jewish Council, move three young, alleged food smugglers through a crowd in the Warsaw Ghetto, 1941. Adam Czernaikow (the well-fed man wearing the fedora at right), head of the ghetto Judenrat (Jewish Council), observes the proceeding.

Ghetto Fighters House Archives

and turned my backside red and purple. My father cried and begged the guards to allow him to stop. When the torture was over, my father carried me home and I ended up in bed and in pain for several days. The moment I showed improvement, it was back to the construction site, laying bricks.

Though now a young man of eighteen years, I looked much younger because of my small stature, only five feet four inches tall, and down to just 130 pounds. My orange hair and fair skin easily gave me the look of a boy about fifteen. Later, with more weight loss and some cunning deceit, I was able to appear even younger—a ploy that would aid my survival in the years ahead. In fact, so fearful was I to divulge my true age, that I thoroughly invented a new age for myself, signing all documents with a date of birth that would have me three years younger.

At the construction site, our food was cooked by Jewish women on kitchen detail, and we all lived together in one barrack, sleeping on straw mattresses strewn on the floor. One night I woke up feeling chilly and my body was itching all over. It felt like it was on fire. God, what was happening to me? At work the next day, I was itching uncontrollably and blisters appeared

between my fingers. I was told I had a sexually transmitted disease, which was impossible because I never had any relations with women. Other boys suffered the same thing. We were given a foul-smelling cream to use on our skin four times a day. I believe that scabies or lice were invading us from those straw mattresses.

Eventually we returned to our families in the ghetto, where the Germans mostly left us alone. We tried to go on as before, celebrating weddings, bar mitzvahs and births. When there was no work we teenagers had nothing to do, so we found solace in each other. Some of the boys had girlfriends, or we just had friends we could kid around with, which helped take our minds off our uncertain fate. It was comforting to be together but even our fun was tinged with fear. Idleness and fear do terrible things to the human soul. We all did a lot of praying, as Jews have always done. It was our only defense against German control and the lonely despair of the ghetto.

Rumors were everywhere and all the time. Some said we would be shipped to Germany. Others said we would be shipped off to work camps or to other ghettos. No one knew for sure. And then one day it happened. Not surprisingly, the Nazis chose a Jewish holiday to give the order.

Humiliating Jews was good sport for the Nazis. In Łódź, Poland, September 1939, a religious Jew, seated in a wagon and wearing a prayer shawl, is forced to bear the sign, "We wanted the war and that is why we suffer." On the wagon is written "The Jews are our disaster."

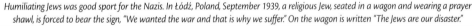

Yad Vashem

Tish B'Av is supposed to be a solemn day of commemoration, but for me it will always be a time of great personal sorrow. It was in August 1941, when I was separated from my family forever. On the morning of this holiday, my mother and I were the only ones home. My father had been called to work, my sisters were doing light work in the square and my younger brother was playing outside. Lying on the couch, my mother was quite ill and in pain with her ulcer kicking up, when we heard the announcement crackle over the loudspeaker. "We need two hundred boys between the ages of ten and eighteen immediately!" I began to tremble. The two of us huddled in the room together in stunned silence listening to the commotion outside, and we prayed to be left alone. Suddenly there was a knock at the door. Neither of us moved, we barely breathed. A large man kicked the door open and stood there with his snarling shepherd dog. He asked me how old I was and pointed out the door—"*Jude 'raus!* Get out Jew!"

I grabbed a little bundle that my mother had prepared for emergencies with food and clothes. Then he grabbed me by the shirt and shoved me out the door. I saw trucks ahead waiting to be

In the Warsaw Ghetto, an SS man barks out orders for young men to mount the truck that will take them to their work assignment—or perhaps to a labor camp, 1940. – Ghetto Fighters House Archives

loaded with human cargo, and the soldier pushed me forward while I cried hysterically, not just for myself, but for my sick mother. As the truck began to move, I watched in disbelief as she came running after us. She chased the truck for about a hundred yards until the SS officer raised his gun and sprayed machine gun fire all around her. It was so confusing and terrifying. There were shots and screams then a cloud of dust. She dropped to the ground but I didn't know whether she was hit or fell from exhaustion. I only saw a small figure lying there, a fading dot as we drove on.

It was the last time I would see my mother.

A look into the faces of young Jewish boys and men being rounded up for labor detail in the Warsaw Ghetto, 1940.

Zagórów

The Zagórów Ghetto was established May 15, 1940, when the first Jews arrived from Slesin. Property was confiscated, men and boys were forced into labor, and all Jews were required to wear white armbands. Soon, Jews from Wilczyn, Konin, Golina and other cities followed, and by the end of that year the Jewish population reached about 2,000. People were packed into houses with other residents but were required to leave their luggage in storage at the church or fire house. After liquidation, their belongings were exported to Germany.

Zagórów was an "open" type ghetto—Jews could move freely through the streets but could not leave town. Both Jews and Poles performed forced labor, and children strong enough to lift a stone were forced to lay stones in the road. When the Nazis burned down the synagogue, Jews were forced to clean up the remains.

The last group of forced laborers, about 450 men, was dispatched from Zagórów in August 1941 to the salt mines of Inowrocław. By October, the remaining Jews of Zagórów were taken into the forests near Kazimierz Biskupi, forced to dig their own graves, and executed with guns or gas. Zagórów was then declared "Judenrein," or "Jew-free." This following account is taken from eyewitness Mieczysław Sękiewicz[3]:

> The Nazis ordered the crowded Jews to take off their clothes. . . . The screaming and crying were beyond description. Some of them threw themselves without even being forced, others, who put up resistance, were beaten and thrust into the ditches. . . . Two Gestapo agents pulled the hose from the engine to the big ditch, started the engine and began pouring something on the Jews crowded in the ditch. . . . The scream of people was so indescribable that we, who sat near the clothes, tore the rags and stuffed our ears with them. The yelling of those boiling below was accompanied by the crying of the Jews who waited for their deaths. This lasted about two hours or even longer."

A Zagórów Survivor

Leon Jedwab is one of a handful of people who survived the Zagórów Ghetto. He was a resident of Zagórów before the ghetto's existence. In 1940, Leon and his family were told that they should prepare space for Jews coming from other towns. Before the Jews arrived, police entered his house, demanding they vacate the premises. A group of German women accompanying the police quietly went about the house selecting furnishings that appealed to them. The police then placed stickers on each item, requisitioning them for expropriation.

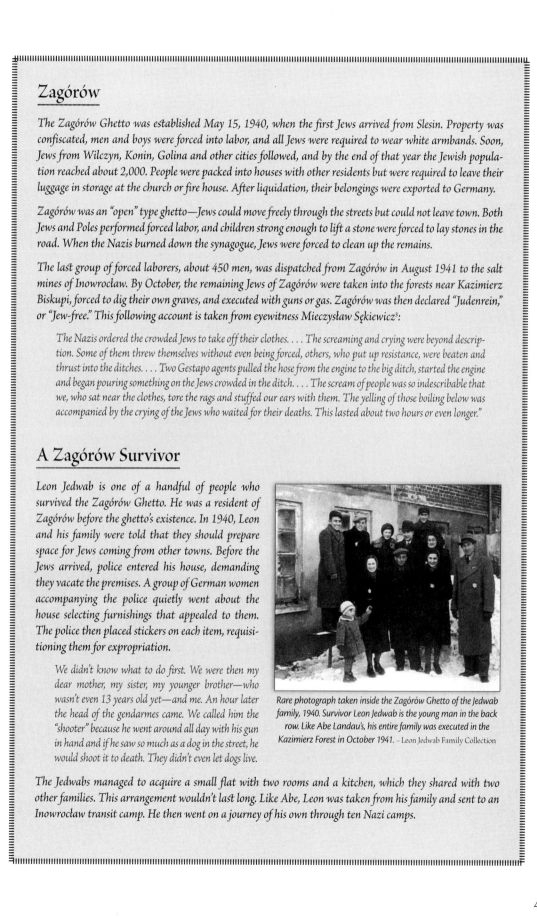

Rare photograph taken inside the Zagórów Ghetto of the Jedwab family, 1940. Survivor Leon Jedwab is the young man in the back row. Like Abe Landau's, his entire family was executed in the Kazimierz Forest in October 1941. – Leon Jedwab Family Collection

> We didn't know what to do first. We were then my dear mother, my sister, my younger brother—who wasn't even 13 years old yet—and me. An hour later the head of the gendarmes came. We called him the "shooter" because he went around all day with his gun in hand and if he saw so much as a dog in the street, he would shoot it to death. They didn't even let dogs live.

The Jedwabs managed to acquire a small flat with two rooms and a kitchen, which they shared with two other families. This arrangement wouldn't last long. Like Abe, Leon was taken from his family and sent to an Inowrocław transit camp. He then went on a journey of his own through ten Nazi camps.

Remnants of Nazi fortifications still litter the countryside along the cobblestone "highway" through Rąbinek from Inowrocław, 2011. – Photograph by Jarosław Buziak

CHAPTER IV

INOWROCŁAW AND RĄBINEK

My journey into a strange and terrifying new life began on this day, in this truck, as we bobbed up and down over dusty, bumpy roads to our first destination, Inowrocław, which was several kilometers away. It was a large city, known for its salt mines and transit station. We later learned it was not a settled camp but a transit camp where you stay until someone decides where you should go. I don't recall its name, but my memory of this place is that we had nothing to do for days and weeks that seemed to drag on forever.

I now feared that I may never see my family again. I was on my own. Our new home was a large barrack with a single light that struggled to illuminate the main room. A wood-burning stove, or *kachelofen*, stood in the middle of the room. That first day we sat at long tables and hungrily ate bread and soup. Afterward, there seemed to be no plan for us, and we stood around and gazed at each other fearfully through the long afternoon. We were well guarded by imposing SS troops with swastika armbands and tended to by Hitlerjugend. The Hitler Youth were young teenagers, like many of us, and they ran around in their clean, pressed uniforms like servants who couldn't do enough for their masters. Eventually, we were divided into groups of ten and sent to our rooms—tiny rooms with three bunk beds. We were given striped pajamas that looked like prison suits, and we slept three to a bed with one boy on the floor. There was no toilet or water for washing—they were outdoor activities.

The first couple of days were just confusing. The younger boys spent their time crying and missing their families while the older ones feared for the future. Most of us walked around in a daze. The guards woke us up early, and then we had nothing to do the rest of the day. Usually we were taken out to a field and left there for hours at a time. Barbed wire surrounded the camp and about twenty SS men walked the perimeter with their dogs. Nobody could think of escaping. Our only duty was to clean up the camp, which didn't take long, so we spent the first few days in the field just walking around and talking. The guards didn't bother us.

After about five days, a new truck arrived carrying two of my cousins. I jumped up and down, I was so happy to see them, and I somehow felt safer with them here. They were older, twenty-five and thirty, and they told me how they were rounded up, same as me, and now we were together, standing aimlessly in a field. We went on like this for about two weeks. Then one morning, we got a rude awakening. At 3 AM, the guards banged on our doors and shouted over a loudspeaker, "*Alle Juden raus! Alle Juden raus! All Jews get out!*" We dressed quickly and went out, then were sent back to the field. This was a drill to force us to dress and respond in seconds.

Those first few weeks in the camp were not so bad. There were no beatings, no shootings, nothing. We had rations three times a day, coffee and bread in the morning, soup with potatoes or a bit of horsemeat at noon, and two pieces of bread at night with a little marmalade.

On one of my last days in the camp, one of the Poles who worked there brought me a large wooden suitcase. The man was from Wilczyn and he said quietly, "Your father gave me this to give to you." Incredibly, my father knew where I was. Inside I found a blanket, two pillows and a beautiful three-piece suit he had made, along with a note: "We are prepared to go away, and we don't know where." This was late September 1941.

The call came for thirty-five boys to go on to the next camp, and I was one of them. We were not certain what day it was when we started out, but I thought it was the Jewish holiday Rosh Hashanah in early October. I was glad I had my prayer book with me. They lined us up in columns of four and told us to start walking. And so we walked. And walked. We didn't know our destination. The suitcase my father sent began to feel heavy and I was feeling weaker. A Czech guard ran over and shouted, "*Schmeiss das heraus, du verfluchte Jude! Schmeiss das weg! Get rid of this, you damned Jew. Throw it out.*"

I took a bold stand and answered him in German, "My father sent it and I want to keep it." This Czech guy was a thug. He was big and surly, wearing glasses that appeared small for his large head and pressed against his fat face. He had a rubber bat, a truncheon, and he beat me on the head, hands and feet. He wanted to find out what I had in the bundle and why I wouldn't throw it out. Then he decided to beat everybody else, too. It didn't slow us down. We walked about five miles and were completely exhausted. We couldn't walk another step when we finally arrived at this desolate place and stopped. There were no homes here, just an open field and a single barrack with the word "Rąbinek" painted on it.

The transit camp Inowrocław Błonia (September 1940) is likely where Abe was held. A subcamp of Stutthof created in March 1940, it also served as a POW camp and a facility for the Gestapo. Because of the scale of terror and brutality that took place here, many Poles consider it a death camp.

Courtesy of Marcin Habel, Szlak Pamięci

Rąbinek

Labor camp[1] Rąbinek was bleak, located in the middle of vast open fields that stretched out for miles. Our living quarters consisted of one huge room with a stove and straw strewn on the floor. There was no running water, just one sink connected with a pipe to the outside of the camp. The toilets were out in the field, about three hundred feet away. We looked around for evidence of food—always a concern—and were told that food would be brought in from another camp at noon. Each boy had a pillow and blanket, and we slept on straw mattresses.

And so began my first experience in a labor camp. That first morning, at 4 AM, we were forced out into the yard for *appell* (roll call). The weather had turned cold and windy, and we stood there for two hours with nothing to do, aching with hunger and from the beatings received on a long march. We hopped and jumped from one leg to the other trying to keep warm. Yet all we could think about was breakfast. Finally, our meager ration of coffee and bread arrived. We devoured it and were quickly corralled into marching columns to be led by SS guards, dogs and machine guns to a work site several miles away. There we were handed over to the *arbeitskommando* (work detail). "We are going to build a railroad," barked the guard. "So get to work, no malingering and no stealing." Actually, we were to build a water refill station for steam locomotives.

That was it. Each boy was assigned his own shovel and pipe and warned not to lose or damage the equipment. Our first task was making railroad ties, and we learned the job by doing it. The big moment of the day came when our food arrived by truck at noon. Soup! That was it—soup. But for us it was a banquet and we gathered around like hungry dogs and sloshed it down.

It was after six o'clock when we arrived back at the barrack looking like coal miners and headed to the outdoor pipes to wash. We had no change of clothes, only the blue shirts we got when we arrived, and for footwear we wore *treppes*, wooden shoes. We worked and slept in our striped pajamas.

The work area, called *gleise* in German, was a large railroad junction where twenty or thirty tracks merged and crossed each other. There were many German engineers working there and Polish workers doing heavy construction, but we were not allowed to talk to anyone. After about three weeks, the Polish workers were gone—their paid labor replaced by our slavery.

The conditions in the camp were not good and some of the boys got physically sick or psychologically beaten down and began to talk to themselves. With no heat or lights, it was always dark and cold, day after day. The guards were sadistic. If we needed to go to the toilet, we were instructed to go to the field and ask permission from the main guard. "*Herr Stumpfuhrer, ich mochte heraus gehen,*" we would say. "Guard, I would like to go out." If he decided to let you go, you went. If he decided against it, he'd order you back to work. He toyed with us, and we'd go almost crazy from the strain of holding it in. Sometimes we were sent back and forth three or four times.

The work became easier and quicker as we did it, but back in the barrack cleanliness was a problem. We hated wearing the same filthy, lice-filled clothing day after day. Along our work route, we had spotted a twenty-gallon tank similar to a gasoline tank, and we thought it might be useful. One night a few of us went out and dragged it in, figuring we could use it to boil our dirty laundry. It worked and we began doing our laundry in the middle of the night.

Our main problem was food. We were desperately hungry all the time, especially after putting in long hours of hard labor. In the barrack, all we could talk about was food—the food we ate at home, the special food we used to have on holidays. Eventually our conversation became more desperate. We needed food. Where and how to get it, we didn't know, but without more food, we could not survive.

Inside the barrack we were left alone and could do as we pleased. Amazingly, there were no guards outside either. The SS lived in a nearby city and went home at night. Once we realized this, we came up with a scheme to bring in more food. About three miles away was a small town, Mątwy, where we could see lights burning in people's homes. Our plan? Every night two boys would sneak out, head off in the direction of Mątwy, knock on doors and beg for food. The idea delighted and terrified us. What if we were caught? We would be shot—it would be quick. But we were going to die slowly if we couldn't get more food. It was worth the risk, and everyone had to be part of it. We all agreed.

In the beginning, things went well. The people were shocked to see us—starving, dirty boys at their doors and they were generous, offering us potatoes, a little meat, whatever they had. For many weeks, we gathered scraps of food and shared it. But the Polish people began learning about the camp's existence and they were suddenly afraid they would be caught. Many no longer gave us food, but we didn't give up. We kept at it until we found a kind soul here or there who would risk helping us.

Why didn't we try to escape? Perhaps if we knew what the coming years had in store for us, we would risk it. But we were young and terrified with nowhere to go. We were afraid of the *Wehrmacht*[2] in the city, afraid of the Volksdeutsche, afraid of the Polish people, afraid

of the SS and their dogs tracking us down. It was a small camp of thirty-five boys, not a camp of thousands. We couldn't mingle in the towns and countryside. We couldn't collaborate—we had no friends and many enemies. The most we could do was show up at random on people's porches and disappear into the night. Sometimes the nights were dark as death, other times the moon brightened our path; occasionally it was freezing cold, but we went out no matter what.

One night I was chosen to go with a boy I had known from the Zagórów Ghetto, and at first everything went as planned. We knocked on doors, and most people said no or were too afraid to come to the door. A few actually started kissing us and calling us poor dears and lost souls. It was a good night—we had a nice bundle of food from about fifteen homes and we wanted to get back and divvy it up.

We knew our way easily by now, through the woods and by a little river, across the field and into the barrack. We crossed the narrow bend in the river, not talking, not making a sound, following the light that would lead us safely back to the camp. Suddenly we froze as we heard the sound of heavy boots tramping back and forth. We stayed low and caught a glimpse. Over there we could

Abe and his comrades trampled across these expansive Rąbinek farmlands in search of food, seen here in 2011.

see him—a guard was patrolling the camp. My God! I thought I'd die of fright and I hunched down so low I backed into the stream with the bundle of food. Submerged in the freezing water, I let the food go. I hardly remember what happened next. I was freezing cold, soaked and delirious. I just remember lying on the muddy bank, so paralyzed I couldn't move. Where was my friend? Had he been caught? At that moment I heard the guard take off on his motorcycle, and my friend immediately reappeared from the bushes. The food was gone. We said nothing and trooped back to camp, ashamed to tell the others we had no food, but a little excited that we had lived to tell about our experience.

We should have been more cautious after this, but desperate people aren't cautious. The next night two boys went out again and the worst happened. A little Polish boy invited them into his house, and when they entered, two German policemen, not the SS, were waiting for them. We never saw them again. The next day the Germans came to our camp and questioned us. "What are you doing? How long has this been going on?" We had to tell them we were very hungry and were trying to bring in food. One of them said, "*Verfluchte Jude, wenn du…Damn Jew, if you do this once more, you will all be shot.*" So we had to stop.

Meanwhile, the small camp was growing bigger. New barracks and homes were being built nearby. The guards were now going to live on site, and in style, so a small village was springing up around us. A new influx of soldiers, guards and policemen would live there, and we witnessed the transition with awe. They had all the amenities— nice homes, heat, food—while things were getting worse for us. The order had gone out to discipline us more harshly, so the guards who arrived each morning picked out a couple of boys to hurt that day and beat them brutally, mostly on the legs. One boy had his legs beaten so badly he was crippled and couldn't walk. He remained that way for some time, until he developed gangrene and inevitably died. He was the first casualty of the thirty-five boys. They buried him behind the barrack.

One particular guard didn't like me and constantly shadowed me. When he tried to start an argument and I didn't argue back, he beat me anyway, breaking some teeth and bloodying my nose. Everyone had their turn as victim at one time or another. As time went on our morale was down, and we looked a mess, all broken and torn up. This same guard approached me later and said,"*Du verfluchte Jude. Ich muss dich tot schlagen!* You damned Jew! I have to kill you." I became afraid for my life and tried to keep my distance from him, which wasn't easy. One day on the work site, he took a shovel and bashed my arm so hard he broke my hand. That night the boys made me a splint, but I still had to work the next day. After this, the guard left me alone and went after someone else.

And so it went at Camp Rąbinek for about half a year. It was April 1942, and they finally decided to build a gallows. I wondered why it took them so long. Yet, it wouldn't take long to put to use. I had a friend from Slesin—a young man about twenty-eight or thirty—from whom I learned a great deal, talking with during evenings. We had been working together unloading rail cars used to transport food, ammunition, cows and other goods. One day he stole some potatoes from the car, hiding them in the barrack. The guards caught him, and soon after, the loudspeaker announced a special event would take place at 10 AM the next day. There would be no work.

That night was eerily quiet. When we arrived in the field the next morning, we looked upon the newly-built gallows. "Line up," came the command, and we stood there, trying not to look and, at the same time, gawking. The silence was broken by SS men on motorcycles who zoomed in, kicking up clouds of dust and grinning as if waiting for the start of a ballgame. They walked over and grabbed my friend from the line, drag- ging him directly to the gallows. The top brass watched from their fine cars. Over the loud- speaker came the warning—"Take notice. From now on anybody who steals will be hanged."

I will never forget what I saw next; it has stayed with me all my life. When they tried to hang him, the rope broke and he lived. This was surely an act of God, I thought, and they will let him go. But no, they replaced the rope and hanged him again. It was over quickly the second time. We filed back to the barrack without saying a word, sick to our very souls. Our camp was down to twenty-nine people. Five had died and one had escaped.

Not long after, we were rounded up in the middle of night and ordered to evacuate the barrack. We did not know what was happening. The mood was low. Many of us had sustained recent beatings and we all had lost a lot of weight. My hand was healing, but I couldn't grab anything with it yet. I had lost four teeth and my nose was swollen and filled with blood. Everyone felt like I did, miserable, losing hope.

We were led directly to the train, all twenty-nine, and pushed into one boxcar. We were never told anything. We were leaving Camp Rąbinek for who-knows-where. We felt fear and sadness. As bad as this camp was, the next one could be worse. It didn't matter. The train chugged along for several hours, traveling over sixty miles to a place the Germans called *Gutenbrunn*, which was located about three miles outside the city of Poznań.

A 1941 German ordnance map shows Inowrocław (Hohensalza in German), Rąbinek (Rombino in German), and Mątwy (Montwy). The camps in this district were either POW camps or forced labor camps, both providing labor for railroad construction. While the existence of a labor camp at Rąbinek is scarcely documented, it is plotted here based on Abe's references to Mątwy and other geographic descriptions.

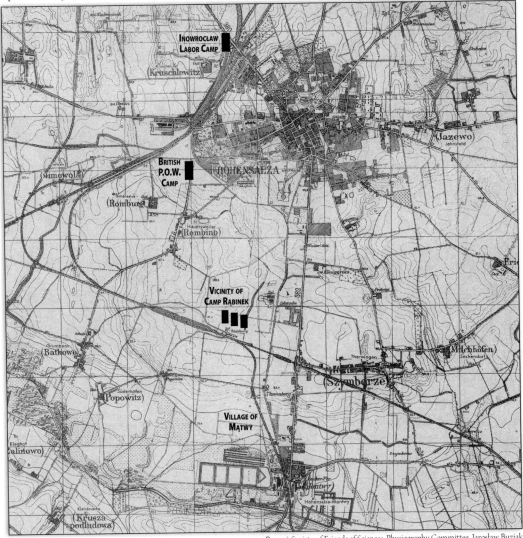

Poznań Society of Friends of Sciences, Physiography Committee, Jarosław Buziak

Inowrocław

Inowrocław, renamed "Hohensalza" by the Germans, was the site of several transit and labor camps, which held British, Polish, and Russian POWs, in addition to Jewish and Polish civilians. Prisoners were put to work on various projects, including a city swimming pool and railway.

Before Abe arrived at Inowrocław, the German army had already made its presence felt. They gathered the existing Jewish population and imprisoned or executed them. By 1939, they had destroyed synagogues, Jewish cemeteries, and other Jewish buildings in the city. By 1940, the entire Jewish population was either transferred to ghettos and camps or exterminated. Inowrocław became a part of the Wartheland province. To make sure their propaganda permeated the city, the Nazi occupiers renamed streets once named for Polish heroes with those of German heroes. For example, avenues named Otto von Bismarck and Adolf Hitler replaced those named for Henryk Sienkiewicz and Maria Konopnicka.

Rąbinek

Before the war, Rąbinek was a large feudal farm-estate with about 35 inhabitants. It was owned by an ethnic German, Rąbinka Benhard Schwersenz, one of the richest men in Inowrocław. Schwersenz turned the land over to the Reichbahn (National Railroad), which built railroad camps there and commissioned the SS to supply laborers to build and expand regional rail lines. Rąbinek was one such camp.

Abe's "Camp Rąbinek" may have become Zwangsarbeitslager Hohensalza-Montwy (forced labor camp Inowrocław-Mątwy), which was part of the military district Stalag XXI. The Mątwy camp existed between December 11, 1942 and August 28, 1943, and was located just about five miles south of ZL Inowrocław (this coincides with Abe's recollection). In 1943, Mątwy was annexed to Inowrocław, and prisoners of war were held here after August until war's end. Because of Abe's testimony, obscure camps such as Rąbinek are not lost in history. Sources: German Federal Archives, Tenhumberg Reinhard, EVZ Foundation, and Lexikon der Wermacht

Rąbinek Station, 2011. This is the approximate location of the Rąbinek labor camp, where Abe and his mates helped build the tracks.

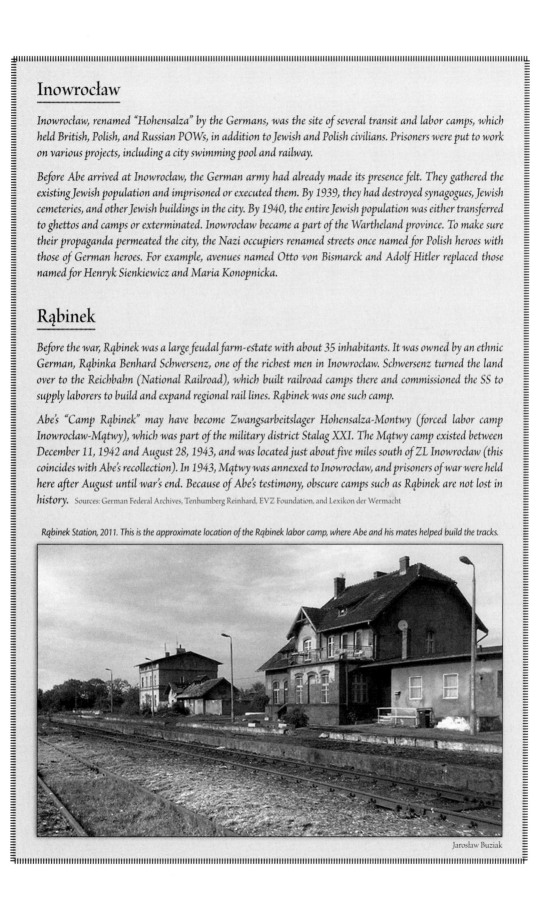

Jarosław Buziak

After the invasion, the Germanization of Poland included the renaming of cities and towns as well as streets, plazas, buildings and landmarks. In this shop outside Poznań, not far from the Gutenbrunn labor camp, women laborers craft German language street signs, 1939. – O. Ang, German Federal Archives

CHAPTER V

GUTENBRUNN AND GLEIWITZ

Labor Camp Gutenbrunn was like a new, unexplored country, where thousands of settlers had set up camp. There were all kinds of people here. The majority were Jewish, age fifteen to sixty, but the very young and the very old seemed to be absent. I estimated that about five or six thousand people lived here, and such numbers renewed my hope that we could find help.

In Rąbinek, we were an all-boy population of young teens, thin and malnourished, with no grown-ups to advise and help us. Our group had become a family—all were Jews from the Zagórów Ghetto, taken from the surrounding cities and towns. Gutenbrunn, on the other hand, was filled with thousands of strangers. Large tents were set up, surrounded by double-barbed wire and watchtowers—so very different from what we had known at Rąbinek! The first thing I noticed was a kitchen, with hundreds of carts and trucks of food being moved from one place or another—they had food here, all right. Enormous containers of soup, maybe fifty gallons, sat in the kitchen. The kids from Rąbinek just stood there and stared at the food.

Without delay we were assigned to a *kapo*[1], or foreman, in charge of our block. The kapos at Gutenbrunn were mostly German Jews, so I thought they would go easy on us, but this was not so. My first kapo, a good-looking, well-educated guy seemed decent enough, but his job was to watch us and answer to the Germans—it didn't matter that he was a Jew. Kapos had made a pact with the devil: To survive they had to please their masters, which meant oppressing their countrymen. Take away the inmates' food? Sure. Keep them idling in the field for four hours? No problem. In exchange for their obedience, kapos received additional freedoms and privileges. Your kapo was your master; some of them were angels—friendly—while others were the very devil—vicious.

At Gutenbrunn, we worked outside the camp. They called this *aussenkommando*. There were no Germans living in the camp itself. The barracks and affairs inside the camp were all managed by kapos. At first, I thought this was a good thing. After all, the kapos were themselves prisoners, but many proved to be as brutal and murderous as any SS or Gestapo[2]. Evil kapos were not hard to find. The one who earned the distinction of being the worst was the Polish Jew who guarded us at work. He was chosen, no doubt, because he was a big, tall guy and strong as an ox. He was also merciless and stupid.

I had just turned nineteen, but was assigned to a barrack of about a hundred and fifty boys between fifteen and seventeen. On my first day at Gutenbrunn, we were marched two-and-a-half miles to a train yard. Our kapo carried his long, rubber truncheon and beat us along the way. At the yard, we had to remove stone, gravel and coal from small boxcars and shovel it all into wagons, which were then hitched to a small locomotive and hauled to some other place. Each person had several wagons to fill and only so many minutes

to do it in. The locomotive soon returned with empty wagons to fill, and the process continued. All day long, we trooped back and forth while they watched us like hawks. It was endless, back-breaking work and breathing in the coal dust made it that much harder. Many of the boys were not strong enough to put in a full day's work and fell or fainted. This meant more beatings by the kapo. He didn't care. He would kill them right there by the wayside, and they would be taken away and not seen again. So if you were beaten, you tried to pick yourself up and continue. If you couldn't, you were dead and dragged away. Perhaps the dead were buried somewhere? We were never told.

When our Polish kapo was assigned to another camp, we were quietly overjoyed. He was replaced by a German kapo who was more lenient and gave us more time to do our job and, occasionally, to relieve ourselves.

Imagine living a life in bunks with so many strangers—some sick, injured, suicidal. It was a terrible time. No one had time to think about anyone else. You had to think about yourself and what was going on around you.

Small-gauge locomotives were used to haul coal, stone and other materials from site to site and camp to camp. The railroads were built by the prisoners. The engine below is being used in excavations near the Crematorium II at Auschwitz Birkenau, 1943.

United States Holocaust Memorial Museum, Otto Dov Kulka

That winter we began a new, more ominous ritual. It was around six o'clock on a dark, cold December evening in 1942 when our kapo ordered everyone to hurry through dinner, come outside and line up in the field. We gulped down our soup ration and hurried outside, just to stand in the cold for about an hour. More than a hundred fifty boys reported in our block alone. Finally, our German kapo came out to check our numbers. He began walking up and down each row, looking directly into the eyes of these pathetic waifs, and snarled as he pointed : "You. You. And you," he said. "And you, you and you." The selection was underway. He chose about thirty people, and the soldiers took them away. In another block, he picked another unlucky group of thirty, and they were removed. We never saw any of them again. Orders had probably come down to thin the growing population, as it was getting crowded, so that's what he did. We thought maybe the chosen ones were going to Auschwitz. We had heard there was a crematorium there, and we knew about Birkenau and Thieresenstadt. We got news about what was going on from people who were constantly coming in from other camps, but we never knew what was true.

And so it went, nearly every day, for the next few months. We lined up after dinner and the kapo chose his victims. At the same time, I carefully planned my survival. I would look this kapo straight in the eye and I'd pray to God—please

don't let me be taken away. Even today, I see his handsome red face staring in my face. It was clear to me that he didn't like sending people away. He was not an evil man. Yet, every night he would select ten, fifteen, twenty boys from our barrack, about two hundred doomed people overall. We knew who they were going to be—the old, the sick, the weak, the bad-looking ones. If someone showed some spirit, he was kept back.

If there was anything good about this camp, it was the existence of food. Here, you could explore, take a chance to steal from somewhere. You could come home with a piece of bread, some crumbs. Near the kitchen, there was a small house with an oven for baking bread. It reminded me of the bakeries in Polish villages— single rooms with massive brick ovens. Without the kapos knowing, hundreds of boys working in the fields picked potatoes and smuggled them in small containers to the oven room, where we cooked them up. Or we'd go to the kitchen late at night and scavenge leftovers and crumbs from food the Gestapo had eaten earlier. It was easier to steal food at Gutenbrunn, but you had to organize yourself. Yes, you had to plan and be smart to risk stealing.

It was also easier to keep clean. There was one barrack with a special room where you could go to take a shower—there were many showerheads and indoor toilets. It also had the bad stuff, including a gallows, an isolation block and an electric gate fence that some inmates would

Kapos stand guard as Jewish prisoners tow rail cars at Płaszów concentration camp in Krakow, Poland, 1943–44.

Photograph by Raimund Titsch, United States Holocaust Memorial Museum, courtesy of Leopold Page Collection

throw themselves against in an effort to end their misery. And there were always kapos who were crueler than others. As we marched back from work, one kapo made us crawl on our hands and knees—fast, then faster—and sing German songs or make animal noises, like a cow or a pig. He did this as we passed through the village in order to humiliate us all the more.

Another kapo, a Polish Christian and convicted murderer, was especially brutal and occasionally made us work at night after working all day. In our bunks and deathly tired, we'd hear over the loudspeaker, *Alle Juden raus! All Jews out!* Five minutes later we were in trucks heading for the train yard. We shoveled coal or loaded products from one boxcar to another for transit to another city. We knew that the faster we worked, the sooner we went back to the barracks. But this man would not allow it. On every boxcar, he swung his truncheon, beating people on the hands, arms and legs. He was a lousy murderer. Each time, we lost four or five boys from exhaustion, and they were taken away. There wasn't a night he went out without leaving behind four or five dead

people. He was so famous for killing that the mere mention of his name filled us with horror.

In fact, death and degradation were everywhere. People were shot as they worked or on their way home. Not one hour of the day passed that I didn't witness death. Cruel death. Sometimes, at work near a field, I would see rabbits running playfully, and I was so jealous, thinking: What right do they have to be free when we have to suffer so much?

I knew nothing of my parents' whereabouts, or the fate of so many loved ones. I had lost my bottom teeth from the beatings. My broken arm, still healing, ached constantly. I was now living without hope. Yet, I was one of the lucky ones. I was strong and good-looking, even without my teeth, and most important, I had good luck. They call this a *schiksal*. I really do marvel over this. How it all happened, I still don't know.

So perhaps it was good luck when in the winter of 1943, about thirty of us boys were put on a truck and transferred to a train on which we traveled for nearly a day, ending up at a camp just over the southern border.

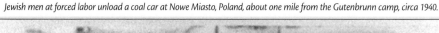

Jewish men at forced labor unload a coal car at Nowe Miasto, Poland, about one mile from the Gutenbrunn camp, circa 1940.

United States Holocaust Memorial Museum, courtesy of Jerzy Tomaszewski

Gleiwitz

Gleiwitz was a heavily industrialized city in northeastern Germany. The camp there was huge, filled with many barracks against a stark landscape; it would eventually become a subcamp of Auschwitz. When I arrived, I met some friends I had left behind at Rąbinek, but we had no time to talk about how everybody was doing. We were split up and brought to the barracks. They told us we would be working in the coal mines in the morning.

It was still dark when they drove us to the mines that first day. Our job was to pick up pieces of coal, load the wagons and push them two or three miles through the shaft. It felt like working beneath the gates of hell. The workers coughed all day, even during breaks, and many did in fact die, right there in the shaft. There were always dead people, all the time. Sometimes I wondered if we were really doing a job or if this was just a way of eliminating people. When the workday finished, we exited the mine in the evening darkness, dirty and hungry.

I was luckier than most. I appeared younger than my age, nearly twenty-one. Having the characteristics of a vital, efficient sixteen year old, and being fluent in German and skilled in various trades, played into my repertoire for survival—which included stealth and cunning. I played these skills to their fullest. I knew what my enemies were saying, and this gave me an advantage. I worked hard and did everything I was told.

We had pretty good rations at Gleiwitz, better than at other camps, probably because the work

"The Thief" and "The Search for Potato Peelings," 1945–49, illustrations by Ella Liebermann-Shiber, a prisoner at Auschwitz Birkenau.
– Ghetto Fighters House Archives

was so hard. They gave us a liter of soup at noontime and another batch of soup before we went back. The soup tended to be watery, but sometimes you'd get lucky and find a piece of potato swimming around. The greatest luxury would be finding a piece of horse meat in it.

Our barrack was relatively clean. The bunks were two and three levels, and each inmate was given a blanket and straw pillow. Stealing was always a problem in the barrack. I wore wooden shoes, which didn't fit, but when I woke in the morning, I often had different shoes, or a different jacket. Usually the thieves left their castoffs behind; if not, we had to try and get a replacement from the supply barracks. Food was never safe. If I saved a piece of bread from breakfast and kept it under my pillow, it would be gone the next morning. I was never able to save anything.

The guards were not brutal, but the work was. People were just dropping like flies. Sometimes you'd be talking to someone and suddenly he'd collapse and that was it; they took him out. Day after day, we went on like this, without much hope. We arrived here in February of 1943, and after a couple of months, we had heard nothing of the outside world.

"A Place of Forced Labor" by David Olere (1902–85). Born in Warsaw and educated at the Academy of Fine Arts, Olere was arrested in Paris in February 1943 and sent to Auschwitz. He was among prisoners who made the "death march" from Auschwitz into Upper Silesia in January 1945. Olere was taken to the Mauthausen Melk camp, where he worked the coal mines near the banks of the Danube. He made over 50 drawings documenting his experiences. – Ghetto Fighters House Archives

It was a strict camp and we weren't allowed to communicate much with one another, but at night, in our barrack, we could speak to a friend, pray together and sometimes play cards. Occasionally, we would steal a couple of potatoes, put them in a container and try to cook them over the steam pipes in the barrack. They were hard and raw but we ate everything. We ate scraps found in the dirt if we could find them. There was no such thing as discarding food.

Now and then, something big did happen. One night we were loading wagons in the mine-shaft and we heard an explosion coming from deep inside, and rocks blocked the entrance so that we couldn't go back in. All those inside were lost. A small cinder from the explosion blew in my left eye and impaired my vision for weeks. It was never treated, and I still suffer from a weakness in that eye. I lost three of my best friends here in Gleiwitz. One died on a "normal" night—he just never woke up—and I wondered for the longest time whether he was sick or had a stroke or what happened. And two other friends were beaten and died from gangrene in their legs. I had a hard time walking by the garbage shed outside the barrack, which reeked of germicide, knowing that dead bodies were kept there for about four hours and then disappeared with the garbage.

Sometimes I didn't know how I could keep doing such hard labor, but I think I worked from fear and so did the others. You had to meet your quota, and if you didn't, you were kept behind to work another two hours. So we had no choice. What I remember most about this time is the darkness, being buried in the mines, never seeing much daylight the whole time we were here.

It was mid-August 1943, when we were informed that we were moving on. Again, with no idea where we were going, we were herded into trains. The cars were closed and practically airless, and we traveled this way for two days, stopping a few times for water. We finally reached a depot and were transferred to trucks. We were back in Poland.

"Working in a Factory in Blechhammer," 1945, by Walter Spitzer. The Blechhamer camp was located just a few miles from Gleiwitz, and inmates from both camps worked for industries such as AEG Gleiwitz, Dyckerhoff & Widmann and the power plant in Upper Silesia depicted here.

Gutenbrunn (Kobylepole)

Gutenbrunn is the German name given to the Polish town of Kobylepole, located on the eastern bank of the Warta River. Forced labor camp Gutenbrunn, opened in March 1940 and closed August 26, 1943. A camp for male Jews, it was one of 32 surrounding the city of Poznań. Prisoners were used by firms such as Philipp Holzmann AG, Green & Bilfinger and Hamann Company for railroad and autobahn construction and the digging of the Lake Malta basin.

In "The Dentist of Auschwitz," author Benjamin Jacobs recounts that the camp was constructed in the typical style of traditional German Junkers' and Polish counts' farm estates: four large buildings arranged in a square with a gate and tower in front. The four buildings, once used as stables, were converted into barracks. The entrance gate was made of wood and connected two concrete buildings, each of which sported small windows with iron bars. The gallows was located near the rear.

> A rusty sign above the gate read "Gutenbrunn." What light entered the room came through windows of iron bars, augmented by an occasional light bulb that hung listlessly from the high ceiling. There was just enough light so that we could see the bunks.... By the time we got to Gutenbrunn, eighteen hundred inmates, all Jews, were already inside the walls. Yet Gutenbrunn had better facilities, including showers and an infirmary. The bunks were roomier, with fresh straw on each with a pillow and pallet. But not even this brought an end to the bugs, although taking periodic showers and delousing our clothes brought some relief. We could not see outside the camp grounds.... Sometimes it seemed as if this was all that was left of the universe.

Before Germany invaded, the village was home to a renowned Polish brewery, Brauerei Kobylepole. When German forces took control of the town, they also took control of the brewery, renaming it "Brauerei Gutenbrunn GmbH." Unbeknownst to the Nazi insurgents, the brewery became the main site of an underground Polish scout troop called Wilda PHM Czeslaw Napierala. Scout troops such as this one attempted to aid Polish and Jewish prisoners by smuggling food or other goods inside camp walls. During the liberation of Poznań, the brewery was severely damaged and had to be closed. In 1945, however, the brewery began functioning again—churning out quality beer until 1970, when it was closed.

Gleiwitz

During the war, Gleiwitz was the site of several labor camps whose prisoners were sent to the coal mines. Most of the coal mined there was used to create carbon black, an agent used in the manufacture of synthetic rubber. In 1944, Arbeitslager Gleiwitz became a subcamp of the Auschwitz system and was divided into four separate camps.

Rare photograph of the Gleiwitz radio station taken before the war. Today, only one tower stands.

Gleiwitz, Germany (now Gliwice, Poland), situated on the country's southeastern border with Poland, was the site of the infamous Gleiwitz Radio Tower Conspiracy, which took place August 31, 1939. This dastardly plot, engineered by Gestapo bigwigs Reinhard Heydrich and Heinrich Muller, was a mock attack on the city's radio tower by Nazi soldiers disguised as Polish insurgents. The soldiers seized the tower and broadcast a short anti-German message in Polish. The purpose was to incriminate Poland and help justify a German invasion. Today, the radio tower remains as the highest wooden structure in Europe.

Jews from Hungary await their fate on the "ramp" at Auschwitz Birkenau, May 1944. After being taken off the train, prisoners were formed into two lines by SS guards—men on the outside and women and children on the inside. The strong were selected for forced labor and processed for internment; the old, young and weak were sent directly to the gas chamber. This photograph is one of nearly 200 images found in "The Auschwitz Album" in the collection of the Yad Vashem Archives. It is one of two known photographic compilations assembled by SS Obersturmführer Karl Höcker, the adjutant to the commandant of Auschwitz. This particular album documents the arrival, selection and processing of a train filled with Hungarian Jews from Subcarpathian Rus in May of 1944—a time when the crematoria were operating at maximum efficiency. A second album was donated to the United States Holocaust Memorial Museum in 2007. – Yad Vashem Archives

CHAPTER VI

AUSCHWITZ BIRKENAU

We were driven a short distance to a massive complex that rose from the countryside like a giant city. This was Auschwitz! We were led off the trucks and alongside trains that were surrounded with people. There we stood with hundreds of people and watched as trains and trucks pulled up, spitting out thousands more.[1]

We stood for hours, waiting, staring in amazement at the mass of humanity. Women and children formed one line, men were directed to the other. Some women were stoic, trying to keep their children calm, others were wailing and beseeching God for help. Rabbis, priests and nuns were among the cargo, calmly awaiting their fate. The trucks were met by SS officers marching around with sticks, observing each person crudely, keeping everyone in order.

The day turned to night, and we were still in line. Bright electric lights cast a surreal glow over everything, as though we were in a movie or a dream. All the while, a small marching band, its members clothed in striped pajamas, played this crazy music. Finally, a large truck pulled up and a huge Gestapo man stepped out. His name was Schwartz, I would later learn—a brutal-looking, ugly man with glassy eyes bulging out from his fat head. He looked like a murderer. Every *häftling* (prisoner) in Auschwitz knew this man. When you came into his hands, your life was finished.

Standing in the light thrown by his truck, he approached the front of the line. With his right arm extended and a flip of his thumb—right, left, left, right—he orchestrated the selection with one simple word. "You," this way. "You," that way. He was making lightning-quick decisions about who would live and who would die. Go to the right—you live to work another day. Go to the left—it's over. An imaginary line separated thousands of people in two broad columns. Those on our side of the line were headed to the barracks. Most of the boys I arrived with were still together. We were not fully aware of our good fortune.

We arrived in Auschwitz on a sunny day and I was surprised to see that it was clean and beautifully landscaped with trees and flowers. For a moment I thought, well, maybe this place isn't as bad as they say, but I soon learned these outer trappings were a disguise for the horror that lay underneath. Auschwitz was like a sprawling big city—urban ghettos, hospitals, a chapel for the guards, nice housing for the commandants—surrounded by enormous factories and a transportation network.

I hadn't realized there was an Auschwitz I and an Auschwitz II (Birkenau), and as time went on, I would be trucked between the two (and several subcamps) for work duty. The camp was segregated into many groups—Gypsies, women, children, handicapped, political prisoners, homosexuals, and so on. I was still passing myself off as a boy. That first day I was assigned to a group of about two hundred teenagers and adolescents, and we were led to a barrack where we stripped down and had all our bodily hair shaved; then we showered and finished in the disinfection room.

Jews from Hungary wait disquietly on the "ramp" at Birkenau, May 1944. They face a selection that will likely send them to the gas chamber, as older women and young children were of little use as slaves.
– Auschwitz Album, Yad Vashem Archives

That night we were all crammed in one hot, sticky room of a cement barrack with no beds or blankets, so we didn't get much sleep. Early the next morning, we had to strip and march from the barracks to the yard at the center of camp. Everyone—three to four thousand men and boys from various countries were arranged in columns, five men per row. We were strangers to each other, but there we stood for five hours—bald, naked, hungry, clutching our meager possessions. If someone fainted he was dragged away.

Selections from Hungarian Jewish transports take place on the ramp at Birkenau, one of three Auschwitz ramps, May 1944. SS doctors make most of the decisions about who is qualified for labor and who is killed immediately. This ramp went into operation in 1942 and was located on the grounds of the Oświęcim freight station, between the Auschwitz and Birkenau camps. It became known as "Alte Judenrampe" (Old Jew Ramp) and is where the majority of the mass transports of Jews arrived between 1942 and May 1944. In the distance is the entrance to the camp.

Auschwitz Album, Yad Vashem Archives

An orchestra of inmates plays for a listening audience near the Auschwitz entrance. Here, prisoners could hear classical music as they marched in and out of the camp. – Ghetto Fighters House Archives

A guard commanded us to throw our possessions aside. Somehow, I had managed to hold onto the bundle sent by my father when I was in Rąbinek. Everything else I had sold to the Polish people for food. It was all I had left in the world—a small knife, a gold coin, a piece of bread and a needle and thread for sewing things into my waistband or pockets for safekeeping.

People threw their diamonds, gold, silver, everything into the pile. I tossed the knife and other objects but squeezed the gold coin into the

bread and held on tight. Confident that I'd be able to hold onto this last shred of my former life, I smiled inside. I wouldn't let go. Suddenly, the guard snatched the bread from me and threw it away. And that was it.

Now I was completely naked, in spirit as well as body. It is hard to explain what I felt after losing these final items. Incredibly, I felt reborn. Free! I no longer had anything to lose—I had lost everything, and now, instead of holding tight onto these pieces of my past, I could focus on my immediate survival and the future. Imagine— reborn in Auschwitz!

In late afternoon we were still standing there in line, and two SS men approached with sharp instruments. One held my arm tight and the other, perhaps a doctor from the Red Cross, tattooed[2] the number 141282 on my left forearm and a small triangle. It was a brutal process, with the branding pen burning into my flesh. My hand swelled. Again, we stood in silence, and in late afternoon, we were taken to another barrack and given blue shirts and pajama pants, a hat and new set of underwear.

After being shaved and disinfected in the "sauna" at Birkenau, a group of men selected for forced labor—Hungarian Jews from the Tet Ghetto—await instructions, May 1944. The look of bewilderment may reflect concern for the fate of their loved ones.

Auschwitz Album, Yad Vashem Archives

The number 141282 was my new identity, and the triangle identified me as a Jew. The Nazis referred to us as *Musselman*[3], or a starving Jew waiting to die. The various kapos in charge—they were also political or criminal prisoners—wore badges that indicated their crimes. A green triangle meant its wearer was involved in politics. The kapo with a black triangle said he was a murderer from Germany serving a life sentence.

The Auschwitz slogan *"Arbeit Macht Frei. Work makes you free,"* was supposed to inspire workers to give their all. But in a strange twist, for two or three weeks, we had no work assignments at all. This welcome break gave us a chance to rest and regain our strength. We spent long afternoons in our quarters, small barracks with just enough room for our beds, blankets and pillow. We were free to wander about but couldn't go beyond sight of the barracks. Meanwhile, the music played day and night.

It was during Tish B'Av in 1943 that something mysterious and awful happened in the barracks nearby. I remember the date because the religious Jews were praying and moaning with their Hassidic books in hand, and it almost seemed like a chorus commenting on the unfolding scene. That hot day, dozens of transports carrying mostly Jews arrived from all over Europe—Romania, Hungary, Germany, Poland. Thousands of children came that day, all boys between five and thirteen, and were assigned to the children's barracks. Since we had no work, we visited them, talking and sharing chocolate rations. Then, a day or two later, everything was quiet. The children had disappeared. We were astonished at their sudden disappearance.

This event was followed by terrible news from some newly arrived people from Poland who had known my parents. They said my mother and father had been gassed by the Nazis in the woods near Zagórów not long after I had been taken away. My good parents—gassed! I felt sick, and yet such news did not register at all. The full impact didn't touch me. I was completely numb and not really sure what had been said—it was all so hazy. Living day to day with such evil, I could not process the worst of it. It went deep

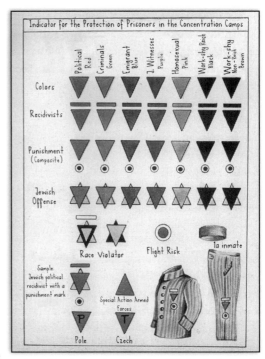

A chart of Auschwitz prisoner markings (digitally edited to provide translation), 1938-1942. Jews wore the yellow triangle, right-side-up. This allowed for the combining of triangles, forming a six-pointed star, while denoting an added offense. For example, a Jewish-communist-recidivist would wear a yellow triangle overlaid by a red one with a bar at the top. The "Work-shy" category included "asocials" such as prostitutes, vagrants, thieves, homosexuals, Gypsies and race violators (committers of inter-racial sex). – United States Holocaust Memorial Museum

inside and disappeared in the gut, and I quietly returned to the business of staying alive.

There was a certain camaraderie in the barrack and that helped us to survive. We learned about each other's views on religion and politics just by knowing where a person was from. We were Polish Jews, German Jews, Yugoslavian Jews, French Jews, and we had much in common, the same hopes and fears. The French Jews were somewhat different in that they were more self-assured than others. They took it easy and couldn't believe they were even in a concentration camp. The Nazis did not favor one group over the other—we were all treated with equal contempt.

In late September, the trains began coming in right through the camps, and it seemed as if things were happening faster. Gazing through the barbed wire, we watched as people were brought from the transport and marched in a column toward the gas chambers. We shouted to a group of them, asking where they had come from. "Holland," they replied. As I looked down the line, I was stunned by what I saw—an uncle of mine with his wife and two children. They had probably fled to Holland for safety, though I hadn't known they were living there. I was too far away to call out to them, but there they were, standing in line, waiting. I began to cry.

At that moment all hell broke loose, as people suddenly realized they were facing certain death. There was crying, shouting, praying. Such an odd mix of people—some Jews wearing stars, Russian soldiers in uniform, rabbis in old clothes, some women in rags, some in stylish coats. For the next several weeks, this scene was repeated every day. People were herded from transports, the SS behind them, whipping them, sometimes shooting at them or over their heads. Some of the people tried to kill themselves by running into the electric fence. In the barracks, people were chanting and saying special prayers, some reciting from tefillins.

What I remember most was the stench and the music. There was a foul smell penetrating the camp you just couldn't avoid. The nearer you got to the crematorium, the worse the smell, which was aggravated by the swampland surrounding the camp. And the music was always playing— loud marching music, German music. The orchestra players were inmates, Germans, Jews and others. There was one verse that the SS sang along with in German: "The Jewish blood will flow into the rivers…"

We knew that when we came to Auschwitz it was the end of the line. No one believed they would ever come out of here alive. I was in Auschwitz a long time—or so it seemed—from the summer of 1943 to January, 1944. Between the main camp and Birkenau, I did all kinds of work—building roads, railroads, structures—I even sorted the clothes that people removed before entering the gas chamber. The nightmare that was Auschwitz lives in my mind. Talking about it has awakened the beasts that torment me. Lately when I lay down to rest, I hear a loud crashing in my head, gunfire rattling my brain

A rare view showing POWs in line receiving soup rations at Auschwitz, 1939. – National Polish Archives

and chaos overtaking me. We were shackled in fear, not knowing when our time would come, always waiting and expecting the worse.

Sometimes when I worked in the fields or factories, I was spooked by my own shadow. I was so afraid of every step, every move I made. I could not bear to see the SS guards walking their dogs around the camp, and I often mistook my own shadow for something creeping behind me. Yet with all the terror, you had to have faith, you had to go forward. Otherwise you'd lose your grip. You had to think, I can't give you that. I had to find a way to keep a vestige of my being.

Just to witness all this, I had to have strength. I told myself, Look, maybe I will get through this, or maybe tomorrow a miracle will happen, and I will get free. The word "maybe" was always in my mind. After seeing so many people die so brutally, it was easy to lose hope, to become too weak in spirit to fight back. Many died from losing hope. We couldn't fight back with weapons, but we could fight with our will to survive.

We would see signs of hope in the skies. Allied planes were flying overhead. Troops were going back and forth over the railroads. Often I asked myself, why aren't the Allies coming to destroy the crematoriums? Why is Hitler able to build this machinery of death? I had been brought up in a devout orthodox family and leaned heavily on my faith. It was always there for me. I never wanted to give it up. I always said, Thank God I'm still alive. Perhaps the day of liberation will come.

My time in Auschwitz was clouded in uncertainty, and I was subjected to constant movement. Transferred to several different

A newly built lazarett in Birkenau, Block B-II f, 1941. The photograph is from a collection documenting construction projects in camps I and II, including the extermination facilities, 1941-1943. Larger camp hospitals were made of brick. – Photograph by Otto Dov Kulka, Yad Vashem Archives

barracks, assigned to many different jobs, I never knew my status, whether today I'd survive or I'd be sent off to the crematorium as casually as I was sent to a work site. I had been working for several weeks, gathering clothes and shoes left behind by people who had met their fate in the crematorium. I treated the sorting like any job and tried not to think about the people who had worn these clothes. Sometimes their clothes even felt warm, or maybe I imagined it.

At this time, an SS man came into Block 40 looking for young men to do bricklaying, and I was among the ones chosen. About two hundred boys who had arrived more recently joined us, and we would show them how to lay bricks. The job lasted for about five weeks, and when it was over I began to worry again. As long as there was work, I might be able to stay alive. Shortly after, another SS officer came to our block and asked for some boys who could speak German well. I raised my hand immediately, and he assigned me and a few others to a *lazarett*[4], a small hospital, to work with Dr. Manne, a French doctor. Dr. Manne was also a prisoner but he was not Jewish. I was to serve as his page, delivering sealed letters, medications, and various items from one place to another. We were warned not to speak about anything we saw.

As jobs went, this was one of the better ones, especially compared to heavy labor. We could move freely through the camp and went back and forth, from barrack to barrack, all day long. The work seemed harmless until the day a pack of

Germans doctors arrived on motorcycles. They had come to work in the *chirurgische abteilung*, the surgery ward, to conduct experiments, as I later learned. Their bait for that day would be boys from one of the barracks, delivered by the man who was in charge of them. Of the two hundred boys in one block, about thirty or forty were singled out the first day and given an injection in their right arms. After a week or two, every boy got sicker and sicker. They died slowly, each differently. Some, their faces changed color, some couldn't eat, some had painful cramps. Some were given injections straight to the heart. Soon all two hundred were dead. One morning a truck pulled up to the block where the bodies were piled and took them to the crematorium.

Dr. Manne was in charge of all the blocks where experiments were carried out. The Gestapo trusted him, and because I walked with him from one block to another, I saw many terrible things. But I had to be careful; Dr. Manne warned me, "Don't ever say anything about what you see here. If you do, and they find out, you'll be shot." So I kept my mouth shut.

I worked for two or three months, running all over camp to places where medical experiments were being conducted. People came from Block 20, Block 61, Block 10, Block 7 and others—suffering from cancer, typhus and malaria—and were injected. In Block 61, I saw people writhing in pain and then taken away. In Block 7, where only gypsies were confined, I watched as twenty to thirty people a day were taken out for experiments. Thousands died in the name of Nazi science.

One day, as I stood outside the block awaiting assignment, a transport arrived with thirty to forty women who were about fifteen to thirty years old. How terrible they looked, their heads shaven, naked and pregnant! I watched as they were ushered inside. Many looked like they were due for delivery. One of the women wandered outside, and I asked her what was going on. She told me quickly they were being operated on, which meant cut, probed, injected.

Ultimately, none of the women would experience motherhood. Some infants were born dead, some born alive and taken away, perhaps for further experimentation. Some of the women were injected as they gave birth.

Meanwhile, I continued to be transferred from one place to another, this time to Block 38, then 39, but I still had to report to Dr. Manne. In Block 39, you couldn't stray far. Every block had its particular people, its own problems and its own kapo. If you went into another block, he would say, "What the hell are you doing here? You don't belong here. Go back to your own block."

Another day, thirty or forty men were brought in, and Dr. Manne wrote a message and sent me off to an office where they kept medications. A German doctor was in charge there, and he answered the message from Dr. Manne and sent me back with a small, sealed box. Dr. Manne opened the box and gave everyone half an "aspirin." The men started crying and acting abnormally. The aspirin must have been laced with something. The men, all Gypsies from Block 7, were watched for four or five days by three people—a German doctor, Dr. Manne, and a third man. Eventually they all died.

Every block was different in its way. Block 8 was a transit place—people came and went. Many were Russian prisoners, but there were people of other nationalities there, too, civilians and soldiers. They had come in from different concentration camps. Dr. Manne estimated that over a period of two to three weeks, twenty-five thousand people went through this particular lazarett.

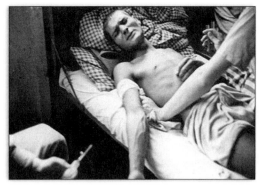

A Roma (Gypsy) victim of Nazi medical experiments conducted in an attempt to make seawater potable. Dachau concentration camp, Germany, 1944. – National Archives, College Park, MD

In Block 10, I came upon four friends who told me the doctors did experiments on men and boys, mostly vasectomies and castration. They said they used no sedatives or anesthesia—the boys just had to endure the pain. Several doctors would hold the victim down, make the incision and remove the testicles. Hearing this story was too much for me. I was very fearful that they would someday call me. I told Dr. Manne how afraid I was. He knew me very well, you know, he was a good friend. He said the only thing he could do was to transfer me to a different barrack with younger boys. However, I must never say anything about where I had been working. I said I would not. I could no longer work with Dr. Manne, nor could I return to that area.

So again I ended up in quarters with younger boys. Nearly twenty-two years old, but scrawny, pale and bald, I was still able to mix in with the adolescents. The two hundred or so teenagers I shared quarters with now needed to be kept busy, so a kapo showed them how to lay bricks. I already knew, of course, and we built a foundation in the middle of a field. It was a waste—it was just to occupy us in cold weather. Or maybe they wanted to show the Red Cross or Geneva that they were treating the boys well and occupying them with useful work.

It was winter 1943-44. I was starting to feel that this was the culmination of my life—a slave to the Nazis. I heard from different inmates that in some of the concentration camps the prisoners were fighting back. I never witnessed this. We also heard about the Warsaw Ghetto uprising, but we really didn't know what had happened.

One day, I saw a couple hundred people standing in line waiting to go to the gas chambers, all half naked and burned on their backs. When we asked why, they said they had been experimented on with sulfur. What could you say? What could anyone say? They were standing in line muttering, "I would like to live." People did whatever they could to calm themselves down. We heard their prayers all day long, some in Yiddish, some in Hebrew. Others sang Yiddish songs, which were very calming. There are special prayers in the books asking God for help, for lamentation and for sickness. Some people felt bereft as they faced death and asked, "Where's God?" and others answered, "Look, you can't question it."

It wasn't all prayers. In Yiddish, we have a lot of curses, too, and you heard a lot of curses coming from the boys. They felt free to say whatever they liked because they thought they were going to die. They would add to their curse: "I hope you burn in hell."

Despite the hundreds of death camps in Germany and Poland, and despite the many creative killing methods employed, Hitler didn't have enough time to kill us all. I do believe if the Nazis had another half-year, or a year, none of us would be left.

Soon enough, my life was about to change again. In February of 1944, a large group of us were led to the train ramp and put on the rails again. We rumbled through Czechoslovakia and deep into Bavaria, traveling over 500 miles in several days. In the daytime the train didn't move, to avoid being bombed, and we stayed heavily guarded by Gestapo and SS—very hungry and cold. At night the train rolled, and we gazed at the sky, watching allied planes fly overhead, while hundreds of German tanks rolled by. We had no idea where we were headed and were only thinking about our own troubles, mainly hunger, and what might happen the next day.

Prisoners in the Aufräumungskommando (cleaning work detail), almost exclusively Jews, sort through personal belongings seized from the Hungarian Jewish transport, May 1944. The sort area, called "Canada" because it was seen as a land of plenty, occupied numerous barracks throughout the camp. The looted property was funneled through a complex distribution network that served individuals and administrations throughout the Reich.

Auschwitz Album, Yad Vashem Archives

Auschwitz I and Birkenau

Auschwitz is the most well known of all the concentration camps. It was the largest and most brutal killing center of its kind. It was also the first camp to make use of gas chambers. Built near the Polish city of Oświęcim, the original complex was broken up into three camps: Auschwitz I (the main camp), Auschwitz II (known as Birkenau) and Auschwitz III (Buna Monowitz).

When prisoners arrived at Auschwitz I, they were unloaded onto a ramp near the prison barrack, then passed through the iron gate and beneath the sign

"Work Makes You Free" hangs over the entrance to the main camp, Auschwitz I, circa 1944. – Ghetto Fighters House Archvives

reading "Arbeit Macht Frei. Work will make you free." In 1942, a ramp was set up at Birkenau, which was designated Judenramp, and used almost exclusively for Jews arriving at the death camp.

Auschwitz I served primarily as a prison for political enemies of the Nazi regime, a camp for slaves, and a killing center limited to small, select portions of the camp population. SS engineers sealed off the basement of Block 11 and gassed a room full of Soviet POWs. Later, a permanent gas chamber was constructed. Auschwitz I was also the site of some of the most infamous medical experiments. In Block 10, Nazi doctors, including Josef Mengele, conducted pseudoscientific experiments on infants, twins and dwarfs as well as forced sterilizations and other experiments on adult men and women. Between Block 10 and Block 11 was the notorious black wall, where executions took place via hanging or shooting.

Birkenau was the largest camp in terms of prisoner population and played a key part in the implementation of the Final Solution. Birkenau had the facilities to function as a true killing center. Four large crematoria were installed at the camp, each with three sections: a disrobing area, a gas chamber and ovens.

The barracks in section B-II of the Birkenau camp, 1944. Originally built as horse stables with 18 stalls to stable 52 horses, these windowless wooden barracks had only a row of skylights on either side at the top for lighting. A chimney duct, which ran the length of the building, inefficiently heated the interior in the winter. Two stalls near the doors at each end were reserved for toilet buckets. Three-tier wooden bunks intended to sleep 15 prisoners were installed to serve more than 400 prisoners per barrack.

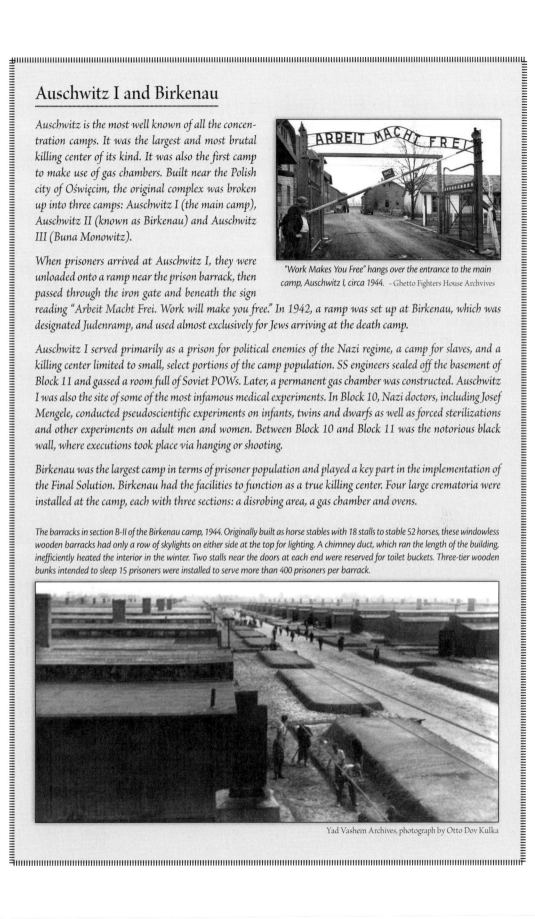

Yad Vashem Archives, photograph by Otto Dov Kulka

Aerial reconnaissance photograph of Auschwitz Birkenau taken by the U. S. Air Force, December 21, 1944. It was among a cache of aerial photographs discovered in the Defense Intelligence Archives by two CIA photo analysts in 1978. The photos were used to plan bombing raids, determine the accuracy of bombing sorties or make damage assessments. The annotations and labels were made by the CIA.

Birkenau, the largest of the three primary Auschwitz camps, also functioned for an extended period as a killing center. It was divided into more than a dozen sections separated by electrified barbed-wire fences and patrolled by SS guards and dog handlers. The camp included sections for women, men and family camps for deported Roma (Gypsies) and Jews deported from the Thieresenstadt Ghetto.

The Auschwitz camps were located between 30 and 40 miles west of Krakow, near the pre-war German-Polish border in Upper Silesia, an area that Nazi Germany annexed in 1939 after invading and conquering Poland. Similar to most German concentration camps, Auschwitz was constructed to serve three purposes: to incarcerate real and perceived enemies of the Reich for an indefinite period of time; to have available a supply of forced laborers for deployment in SS-owned, construction- and armament-related enterprises; and to serve as a site for the elimination of targeted groups whose death was determined to be essential to the security of Nazi Germany. Auschwitz I had a gas chamber and crematorium.

DISINFECTION BUILDING

GAS CHAMBERS IV (DESTROYED) AND V

OT STORAGE AREA

BIRKENAU EXTERMINATION CAMP
OSWIECIM, POLAND
21 DECEMBER 1944

N

FENCE DISMANTLED

BARRACKS DESTROYED

SECTION III BEING DISMANTLED

SS HQ

SS BARRACKS AREA

ENLARGED FROM THE ORIGINAL NEGATIVE AND
CAPTIONED IN 1978 BY THE CIA

KZ Dachau, showing the moat and electrified wire fence, 1945. – United States Holocaust Memorial Museum

CHAPTER VII

DACHAU

The train stopped occasionally during the daytime and we were given water and soup, but not enough. The windows in the boxcars were camouflaged, but I was in the cargo train with open windows and could get a sense of what was happening outside. The war was getting closer.

Nothing was as bad as the packed trains, not even the camps. We were always hungry, and with no facilities we urinated where we were. It was so crowded and cold that people suffocated and froze, finally dropping to form a mat beneath our feet.

Suddenly, the train emerged from the woods and I noticed a sign, "Dachau." It was a mystery to me why so many of us would be shipped to this faraway place. We climbed off the train and into trucks that took us to the camp itself. My memories of Dachau are of exhaustion and doom, overpowering fear and backbreaking labor. For the first few days, we stood behind barbed wire with thousands of others, but soon our work crew began a job up the road constructing a factory with cement. At first I had no shoes, so I wrapped my feet in cloth. The cold seeped in and my feet swelled, making work difficult. I had to have shoes and finally managed to scrounge up a well-used pair.

Going to and from work was as bad as the work; we were forced to march, to sing, to crawl. One particular day will haunt me forever. About fifteen or twenty boys were chosen to work on the tracks, and I was among them. The camp was deep in snow; even the trains were all snowed in. On the way back from the work site, an SS officer was playing around with us, and he suddenly approached a good friend of mine, ripped off his hat and coat and threw them about fifty feet away. My friend didn't know what to do; after a minute, he went to retrieve them. The officer took out his revolver and shot him in the head. Silent and shaking, we watched all this in horror. He then ordered us to dispose of the body, and we left him between the railroad tracks, headless, brains everywhere, turning the snow red. This is one of the worst pictures that has remained in my mind.

This event hovered over us like a storm cloud and terrified us from that day on. That same SS man—a Czech German who always called me *Rote* (Red)—said to me once, "*Du, verfluchte Jude! Ich mach du gerne.* You damned Jew, I really like you." I didn't know how to respond. He always played with my head, and I was quick to do what he asked. At work one day he told me to bring him this and that from here and there, and I was running wildly trying to do as he asked. He seemed attached to me and said again that he liked me. I asked him why, and he said that it was because I looked a lot like his brother. I didn't trust him and tried to stay out of his way. He kept seeking me out and toying with me. This went on for weeks until I left the column.

At a different work site further along the track, another SS man, also a Czech German, was in charge, and he was a good friend of the former guy. They were both from the same town, and we soon discovered the new guy was a hundred percent worse then the other one. He didn't even use a gun to kill, he preferred strangling. If you crossed his path at the wrong time, he'd destroy you. Once we were called out in the middle of the night to unload fifteen boxcars of red bricks. I couldn't go as fast as he wanted, so he bashed me in the face and broke my nose. Back at camp,

By mid-1944, to increase war production, more than 30 large Dachau sub-camps were established near armaments factories in southern Germany. Over 30,000 Dachau prisoners worked exclusively on armaments, many working to their death. – Ghetto Fighters House Archives

I nursed my wounds with cold water and walked around with a swollen nose for two weeks. One day he said, "The biggest pleasure I'm going to have will be on the day I kill you."

At Dachau, I worked mostly in construction—laying bricks, mixing cement, building. It was a short stay but very cold, especially before I got shoes. At that time, my feet were swollen with frostbite and I wasn't able to work fast. I feared that my executioner would drop the hammer any day, as he pushed us to work faster and faster.

Luckily, by April, I was chosen for transfer. Once again I was packed on the cattle train with my fellow workers, headed for the unknown.

This photograph of Dachau prisoners at work was taken clandestinely by Czech prisoner Karel Kasak in 1943. It was printed by Maria Seidenberger, who worked in a photo lab in Munich and whom he befriended. Karel was assigned to photograph gardens outside the camp entrance but secretly captured prisoners at work and around the camp. Maria stored her friend's Dachau photos and letters in her family's beehive and mailed them to his relatives in Czechoslovakia. Maria photographed the execution site of Soviet POWs and the death march from Buchenwald to Dachau.

Source: Interview with Maria Seidenberger, photograph by Karel Kasak, United States Holocaust Memorial Museum

Dachau

KZ Dachau, located in the small town of Dachau, 12 miles northwest of Munich, was the first of the Nazi concentration camps. Established in 1933 as a prison for political opponents of the Nazi Party, such as Communists and Social Democrats, it also served as a training ground for the SS, teaching them how to instill terror in prisoners. Commandants Fritzsch, Hoess, and Kramer were Dachau "graduates."

Pre-war inmates in the Dachau camp haul a roller used in paving roads, 1936. They are being supervised by an SS soldier.
– Ghetto Fighters House Archives

After Krystallnacht in 1938, thousands of Jewish prisoners were brought to Dachau from throughout Germany, marking the first time it was used as a concentration camp. In 1944, KZ Dachau provided outside forced labor to help nearby armament factories increase production. Inmates also built roads, drained wetlands, mined gravel pits, and expanded construction of the camp itself.

Although a gas chamber and two crematoria were built in Dachau, they were never used. Nonetheless, 31,591 of the 206,206 registered prisoners were reported dead as a result of random shootings, beatings, poor conditions or medical experiments.

According to Turkish journalist Nerin E. Gun, when American GIs liberated Dachau, they came upon a grotesque scene—thousands of dead bodies in and around cattle cars outside the camp fences. As SS guards fired into a crowd of prisoners from the watchtowers, the American soldiers quickly fired upon the guards. The SS surrendered and descended with their hands up. Enraged by what they'd witnessed, some soldiers opened fire on the surrendering SS and began to hunt down anyone in an SS uniform. "Within a quarter of an hour, there was not a single one of Hitler's henchmen alive," wrote Gun.

Prisoners on a death march from Dachau move south through the Bavarian town of Gruenwald, April 29, 1945. German civilians secretly photographed several death marches from Dachau, though few of them gave aid to the prisoners.

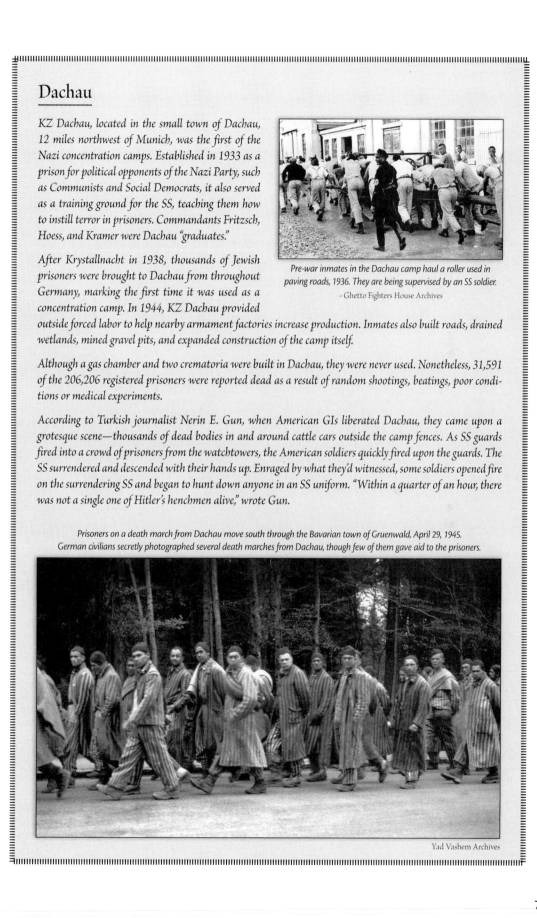

Yad Vashem Archives

Under the watchful eyes of their kapos, prisoners from KZ Buchenwald are hard at work building the Weimar-Buchenwald railroad line. The SS built the railroad in just three months, and it was in constant need of repair. The quick, shoddy work also cost lives. During its construction, one in three camp inmates would die. – United States Holocaust Memorial Museum

CHAPTER VIII

BUCHENWALD

Traveling only at night, it took two days to cover 200 miles, and we arrived at a place that seemed to grow right out of the woods—Buchenwald. At the main gate a sign read "*Jedem das Seine.* You get what you deserve." My arrival in Buchenwald opened a new chapter in my life. Hardened by the events of my life, I rarely spent time thinking about my family. Only intermittent dreams brought glimpses of my loved ones. My thoughts centered around food and survival. It was April 1944, somewhere near my twenty-second birthday.

Here, thousands of people came and went all day long in well organized fashion. The administrators wasted no time in directing us to a big room for showers, which were followed by a white-powder bath that made our skin raw with disinfectant. Our hair was clipped short. Then a number was written on my left breast. I don't remember the number because it was of no concern to me. Our Dachau clothes disappeared and we got new striped uniforms, little hats, underwear and used leather shoes. It felt good to wash and have this clean new outfit.

I kept up the lie about my age, making myself three years younger. One thing about lying—if you live long enough, you begin to believe the lie. For many years, even after settling in Massachusetts later in life, I continued to give my year of birth as 1925. As a prisoner, until this time, I never wavered from this fact and it was never doubted.

I was assigned to block twenty-nine or thirty, with boys seventeen and under, and our first assignment was emptying provisions from the trains and trucks that came in—blankets, food, all kinds of stuff needed in the camp. The work was easy compared to the miserable mines we'd just left, and we could easily steal extra goods from the trucks. But the situation wouldn't last.

After disinfection, the inmates are registered by the staff at Buchenwald. – United States Holocaust Memorial Museum

Roll call, 1941. Often, roll call meant standing for several hours, twice a day—a severe torture in itself. – Yad Vashem Archives

One day, after about three weeks, we were organized into a line of sixteen people or so and marched outside the camp where we emptied bricks and construction materials from the arriving trucks. A brutal SS guard stood over us, beating our legs and heels with a club so we would walk faster while carrying these heavy loads. We went back and forth, faster and faster, and had no time to think. A friend walking behind me with a giant load of stones fell, and the guard shot him right there on the ground. It was awful to see this, a graphic reminder that we'd better keep up the pace. Whenever someone fell, he got shot. When I saw this I thought, My God, they're just going to shoot all of us—like lame animals.

I didn't notice any kapos at the camp. It was all driven by the *Wehrmacht*. But I did notice the camp was growing rapidly. Every day, transports were arriving with thousands of male prisoners— from very young to very old. There was no gas chamber or crematorium, but the killing went on day after day. Most transports arrived in the black of night, breaking the silence with the thunder of trucks and the wailing of humans. This made us more afraid. We were afraid of sound and movement. If a moving shape caught the corner of your eye, you thought they were trying to kill you.

The wooden barracks were like any other place. There was a barrack for dead bodies,

Washing and shaving newly arrived Polish prisoners in the Buchenwald concentration camp, 1940.

United States Holocaust Memorial Museum, courtesy of Robert A. Schmuhl

and a small infirmary barrack where medicine and bandages were dispensed. The rations in Buchenwald were also typical—soup. We would rise at four o'clock in the morning and stand outside for two, three, four hours, awaiting our fate—just standing, standing. This was very hard.

Luck stayed beside me at Buchenwald. One day, while unloading bricks and stones from railroad cars into trucks, I became so tired I thought I would pass out. I just couldn't take it anymore. I wasn't thinking clearly, and in a daze I just drifted away. Soon I found myself about fifty yards from the gang, but no one saw me. So I just crawled under the train for five minutes to rest. This was an involuntary and careless act. The guard didn't see me go, but on the way back, he caught me. "Where the hell you been?"

"I've been unloading bricks up the way." He swore at me violently, adding "Get back to work goddamn Jew." He could have shot me right there. But for some inexplicable reason, he didn't.

When we returned to our barracks, tired and hungry after a day's work and all this horrible pain and pressure, I broke down. The feeling of my body and spirit being in some lunatic's hands had paralyzed me. The man was, absolutely, not a human being. And I found myself praying to God that I would just like to die. Just to get away from it all. But instead I found that the human being is stronger than iron. It can take a lot of stuff.

I now had enough experience with concentration camps to know a few things: The rules in each camp were not made by the Gestapo or handed down from above—every camp made its own rules and had its own way of killing people.

The weak, the old, the young were dispensable, and as thousands arrived every day, many were quickly disposed of. Some were killed as punishment, some for sport, others for no particular reason whatsoever. For example, I saw one man get stabbed because he was wearing newspapers underneath his clothes for warmth—a common practice.

The workers were in another category, but we weren't entirely safe. We could be worked to death. If you were strong and healthy, you had a chance of surviving because the Nazis needed the Jews. They used the Jews to build their society. We built their factories, their houses, their railroads; we built everything. We were a major

"Hard Labor in Buchenwald," drawn by Walter Spitzer during the war. In January 1945, Spitzer, like Abe Landau, walked the death march from Auschwitz to Upper Silesia. He ended up at Buchenwald, making clandestine drawings such as this scene, which describes events as Abe remembers them. After Liberation, most of Spitzer's camp drawings were lost when the camp was liquidated. Today, his art is exhibited worldwide.

Ghetto Fighters House Archives

A hanging at Buchenwald. One victim recalled, "There was a jolt and I was hanging from my arms in mid-air. The beast disappeared, leaving me to my fate. . . ." – H. Stein; United States Holocaust Memorial Museum

Whipping Jewish prisoners at Buchenwald, 1943. After flogging, inmates were assigned to "delinquent company," receiving harsher work assignments under more brutal conditions. – H. Stein; Yad Vashem Archives

part of rebuilding the German Reich! We were helping the Nazis liquidate ourselves. When you could no longer help, you were nothing, finished. This went on in all the camps until the day I was liberated.

Our work schedules at Buchenwald were changed daily, and I never knew where I would be next. I remember one day when we were working in pairs, cutting down small trees in the woods and piling the wood. We had not eaten since morning and by late afternoon, we were starving. The guard generally watched us with his beady eyes, but he would wander off at times, returning to count just how many trees we'd cut down in his absence. While I thought he wasn't looking, I noticed some wild nuts on the trail and couldn't help but pop a couple in my mouth.

Back in the barrack, the guard called me out. "Hey, Red, what did you steal?" He always called me Red. I told him that I'd eaten some nuts because I was hungry. What could I say? "Bend down," he yelled, so I bent over and he gave me four or five lashes with a whip. My buttocks were on fire. I retreated to my bed like a wounded animal. I thought that was the end of it, but a half-hour later he called me back and said I had committed a crime. He had me taken outside the camp to a small pond and pushed me in. He then threw sticks in the water and told me to "fetch" like a dog, using my teeth. I was in the water maybe twenty minutes retrieving the sticks. He was just humiliating me, for sport. I was lucky he didn't shoot me. I thought, for certain, this is the end for me. Other people were getting

killed for nothing, swatted down like flies. I was walking around all the time in the hands of fate. Everywhere I went I felt God watching over me. Would I live or die?

I learned something about human nature in the camps. Seeing so much death, destruction and terror, you learn to be an egoist. You think about yourself and your own survival and less about the fate of others. You fight your friend for that extra bit of food and he fights you. You no longer have any dignity. Dignity is for people who are safe and eat regularly.

One day we were coming back from work detail, frozen and tired, and we checked in at the SS barrack before returning to camp. Outside the barrack was a pile of ashes and coal from burning stoves. The SS came out and said, "I have a whole bag of cheese pieces here," and he took out a handful and threw them in the ash pile. About fifty people went after the cheese— wild, they went wild trying to put something in their mouths. I thought they looked like tigers, destroying each other over scraps of food. A cloud of dust rose from the ashes and when it settled, a few people had some cheese, but most didn't. They were all filthy from the coal dust.

After about two and a half months, we were abruptly told one day that we were going to another camp. There was no time to think about it or brood. We had no idea where we were going, and that very day we found ourselves in cattle cars, packed in like sardines with other weary, despairing people—most living, a few dead. We were used to stepping over the dead by now.

Buchenwald

Konzentrationslager (Concentration Camp) Buchenwald was the third major camp in the Nazi system, opening in July 1937. The name Buchenwald, meaning "Beech Tree Forest," was given by Heinrich Himmler. Situated about five miles north of Weimar, Buchenwald originally served as a prison for German political prisoners. However, the camp grew rapidly to meet the demands of the Final Solution. In its eight years of existence, 238,980 prisoners passed through the camp and its satellites—of these 43,045 perished.

A glimpse inside the barracks just after Liberation.
~ United States Holocaust Memorial Museum

One of the 15 brick buildings in the camp was Block 46, the "Hygiene Institute" of the Waffen-SS. This block, separated from the rest of the camp by a fence and a separate entrance, contained a laboratory where physicians conducted various experiments on inmates.

On April 11, 1945, the day that American troops arrived to liberate the Buchenwald camp, the Communist resistance fighters had already taken control of the camp and forced the SS guards to flee for their lives. The American liberators observed that some of the resistance fighters were hunting down the SS men in the surrounding forest. The SS soldiers were brought back to the camp and shot, hanged or beaten to death by the inmates while the American soldiers looked on and sometimes joined in. [Scrapbookpages.com, H.E.A.R.T]

View of Buchenwald shortly after Liberation, taken from the tower over the main entrance gate. Only about one-third of the barracks can be seen. Able-bodied prisoners in the foreground await transportation to Displaced Persons camps, where they will be processed prior to repatriation. American soldiers in the picture are making a tour of the camp.

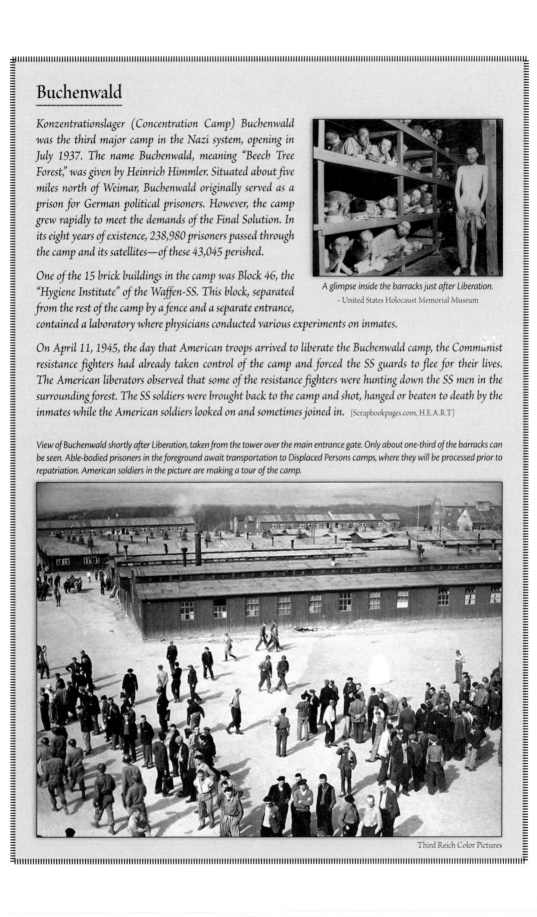

Third Reich Color Pictures

Jews wearing armbands are forced to sweep a street in Będzin, circa 1940.
- United States Holocaust Memorial Museum, courtesy of Benny Hershkowitz

CHAPTER IX

ŁAGISZA AND BĘDZIN

It was nighttime when we pulled into Łagisza, a subcamp of Auschwitz in southern Poland. Though our barracks were here, we were trucked daily to nearby Będzin, where they were building an enormous industrial park. Będzin had been almost 90 percent Jewish before the war, but no Jews lived here now—that time was past. It was now a German machine.

We went to work immediately at a factory building thick metal plates and putting them together. We had to learn to use a lot of new machinery and gadgets. Once I was working ten feet up helping these German engineers, and I felt almost professional. We were constantly lugging equipment into the factory or lugging stuff out. There was plenty of work—cement work, brickwork, loading this, unloading that, making ammo, helping with the war effort. I felt secure when there was lots of work. The Nazis needed workers too badly to kill all of them.

The camp itself in Łagisza was an internment camp, and the first problem I detected was that it had such a small kitchen, considering there were so many prisoners. Nothing was more important to the inmates than a kitchen, but in this place, they had to truck in most of the food, which meant we couldn't steal any. There were many Russian prisoners here, POWs and regular inmates. We had only been here about six days when one of those incidents occurred that you remember forever.

It was dinnertime, and fifty-gallon containers of soup were being brought in as we stood waiting in line, ravenous. When the officers left the scene, two of the Russians slipped into the truck, took two containers and spilled them on the ground. We couldn't believe what we were seeing. They grabbed some potatoes and ran off while the soup soaked into the ground. The officer returned and threw his hands in the air. "Who did this?" The place was quiet.

He became enraged and lined the Jews up on one side of the room, the Russians and Yugoslavians on the other. Meanwhile, they caught the two guilty men, but that didn't matter; every Russian had to pay for the crime. "You'll get no soup tonight," the officer growled at the astonished Russians who had done nothing.

Then he turned to the Jews and yelled even louder, "*Verfluchte Juden, du mussten alles eten!* Damn Jews, you will have to eat it all up!" Our stomachs had shrunk to nothing, and now we had to eat these enormous quantities of soup. We wolfed the stuff down at first, then brought it to a trickle until we thought we would explode. It took a couple of hours. The Russians stood on the other side watching us, wild with hunger. They were shouting and cursing us and fighting among themselves. A normal response, considering they had been waiting for a bit of food all day. This was the Nazis' way of punishing everyone, and their little circus wasn't over yet. The next day they deprived the Jews of soup and force-fed the Russians. About fifteen people got very ill.

The Nazis harassed us day in and day out. One afternoon, a kapo took us out to unload a train and warned us we had to do it fast. He was tyrannical the way he watched us work, looking on like a madman—as if he couldn't wait to beat the first one who didn't meet his standards. I was having trouble doing the heavy unloading of bricks, and I had a feeling about this guy, thinking something bad was going to happen. That night, in order to avoid working the next day, I asked a friend to break one of my fingers. He did, and I was sent to the infirmary, bandaged up and put back to work. Not satisfied, I asked my friend to chop off the top of one of my fingers. He did, then took me to the camp hospital, where they bandaged my finger, and I stayed home for a day. This was the price for one day off—a chopped finger. But these were among the tactics of survival—intuition, premonition, luck.

Two friends I had met at this camp were severely beaten that day and had open wounds all over their bodies. Soon after, they were taken into the middle of camp and hanged; I never found out why. The Nazis forced a Jewish

"An Extra Portion" by Naomi Judkowski, 1945, depicts a scene similar to what Abe witnessed with the Soviet POWs—forced-fed inmates, tortured and humiliated. The text reads: "'You got too little soup? This evening you'll get an extra portion.' Thus promises Schultz, the forced-labor boss. 'Here's what the extra portion looks like.'" The watercolor from Judkowski's album, "The Oświęcim Death Camp," was used as testimony in the Eichmann trial.

prisoner to be the hangman, and afterwards, they left the bodies hanging for two hours. Later that month, a small group of Czechoslovakian prisoners tried to dig a small tunnel from the barrack. They were all caught and brought to the gallows. Tables were placed in the camp yard, which the captured Czechs were forced to stand upon with the rope around their neck. One of the SS guards walked around and tipped the tables. Before they fell, the Czechs were singing "Down with Nazism." They were all hanged. This was Łagisza, 1944.

Sometimes I wondered how I could be so full of faith while witnessing all these horrible things. I don't know. I ask myself this question even today. I could have died not once but a thousand times. It seemed to me that the more people the Nazis killed, the greater was their sense of accomplishment. We understood that getting rid of us was crucial to the success of the Reich, whether by shooting, hanging, gassing, burning or sheer exhaustion from work. Sadly, we had become used to working amongst the dead.

One night the Nazis came into camp with a loudspeaker and announced they were looking for boys who could sew. It seemed like better work than unloading bricks, so I raised my hand. About twenty of us volunteered. In the morning the guards arrived and we thought we were being trucked to a sewing factory. To our surprise, we were taken not far from Łagisza into a deep, dark tunnel only partly built. Our sewing job was to finish building a railroad tunnel!

This was one of my worst jobs. Every day we were up at four, rising in the dark and setting off to endless hours of work in an airless tunnel. I don't believe we saw light for a month. We removed dirt, loaded and unloaded stones and moved around machinery as we coughed and gasped for breath. It was extremely hard work, and not a day went by when we didn't lose a dozen people. They harassed us for being too slow or too fast, and many died of beatings or exhaustion.

We worked there for about two months until an explosion brought an end to our work. These tunnels were so unsafe. We were not inside the tunnel at the time, but some of the workers were. Hundreds of bodies were later removed. We were left with nothing to do for a few days but wait for what was coming next.

Generally we were given rations three times a day but sometimes they didn't give us anything. In camps that had kitchens, we planned our evenings around hunting down food. We could organize ourselves, make trades and split the goods. Here there was no food to steal, and that was very frustrating. Soup arrived in containers at noontime, already cold, and a ration of bread came in the morning. Some people consumed their bread ration immediately, others cut it in half, hid a piece under their coat and finished it at night. But I had learned not to save my ration. When I received it, I ate it. I recall one friend next to my bunk who stockpiled rations for several days, keeping them under the bed—until the day they disappeared. I think you were much better off to eat it right away. I was stronger and had a little more energy.

Once in a while you'd have the opportunity, for a couple of minutes, to talk to people who came in on the transports. I asked one of the girls where she was from, and she told me a story. The girls in her group, German Jews, were taken from a Polish ghetto and sent to Auschwitz, where they became the subjects of medical experiments. Repeatedly raped and forced to perform sexual acts, about seventy girls became pregnant from German soldiers—this was the plan. Once pregnant, they were monitored every day and given injections and blood tests. When they arrived here, they were four, five and six months pregnant. The girl who told me this was from the area, a beautiful girl, even though she had no hair.

Occasionally we worked in the fields and they worked next to us, tilling the soil with a shovel or a stick; others worked on the railroads using a special hammer to beat the stones, heavy hammers, and this was a punishing thing. Some girls were large, and others, you couldn't tell they were pregnant. Some wore handkerchiefs over their heads. After four or five weeks, they disappeared—just like that. I have always wondered what happened to them.

Będzin

After about three months in Łagisza, a small group of us were taken by truck into the city of Będzin, just a few miles away. There was a small camp right in the middle of the city, surrounded by four or five watchtowers and fenced with barbed wire. Imagine this. Right in the city! It looked abandoned but obviously wasn't. The food we were getting in Łagisza was coming from this camp. I was assigned to work in the kitchen making biscuits! This was incredible luck, and I was thrilled. I worked there all day long in two kitchens, and I was sure I'd be able to take food back to the barracks. But the guards were changed three times a day, and they watched us like hawks. We couldn't touch anything. They didn't trust us—they thought we might poison the food.

One kitchen had the most modern facilities imaginable, with coal heat, electricity, clean floors and shining counters. This was the kitchen for the SS and Gestapo, and then there was the other more primitive one for the labor camp. We had to clean the dishes, scrub the pots, make everything shiny clean. Every day, the finest steaks, fish and lobsters would appear from somewhere. We watched all this, and here we were, peeling the potatoes, grateful to eat the peelings, if only we could. But even so, I knew I was lucky to be working in a kitchen. And I soon learned it was a job with benefits.

We could leave when the kitchen was closed, around 6 PM. Since it was dark and we were unguarded, we took potato peels, cheese scrapings and brown apples, all the rejected stuff, and filled a barrel and lugged it back to camp. Here we spread it around to about fifty people and they gave us items in return. One fellow gave me soap, another gave me a needle to sew a button; we had a really good system going. We did this night after night. Sometimes all we had in the barrel were bones—a dog wouldn't eat some of this stuff—but to us it was a banquet. While I worked here, I had some peace of mind. I was not harassed. It was a very rare time for me and it gave me back some of my strength.

It was now late summer of 1944 and there were rumors in the camp that the Allies were surrounding Europe. We saw hundreds of planes flying overhead, and we looked at the sky and prayed that maybe, maybe, a miracle was coming, and somebody would liberate us. Maybe somebody would open the camp and we could get away. But nobody came except the SS men sending us to our next destination.

Prisoner workers in the Dachau camp kitchen after Liberation, 1945. Being on a kitchen detachment was among the most bearable forced-labor assignments in any camp. At Buna, for example, about 40 prisoners were allocated to work in the potato-peeling kitchen, the prisoners' kitchen and the SS kitchen. An additional four or five prisoners, called SS-kalfaktoren, reported directly to the SS and worked as general servants.

Yad Vashem Archives, courtesy of Svetozar Gucek

Łagisza and Będzin

Łagisza is located in the northern district of the city of Będzin in East Upper Silesia. The first Jews to arrive at KZ Łagisza at the end of 1941 were sent by Organization Schmelt to construct "Walter," a power plant with a projected output of 300 megawatts. The builder, Energie-Versorgung Oberschlesien, also employed private citizens classified as "skilled workmen," who were paid four Reichsmark per day, and "helpers," paid three Reichsmark per day. Survivors could later use these figures to be compensated for their labor.

The prisoners at Łagisza also built the railroad that would serve the power plant and worked on other construction-related tasks. In September 1943, Łagisza became a subcamp of Auschwitz, and by November, the number of workers at the Walter power plant exceeded 500. At the time of Abe's arrival in May of 1944, the camp's population had swelled to over 1,000 prisoners.

Before occupation, Będzin supported a thriving Jewish community of about 28,000. Five days after the Germans occupied the city on September 4, 1939, they set fire to Będzin's Great Synagogue, which took 50 adjacent houses in its inferno. As elsewhere, legislation forced the Jews to relinquish businesses and property, but an active Jewish Council helped make life in this "open ghetto" somewhat better than elsewhere in Poland. As a result, thousands of Jews from central Poland sought refuge in Będzin.

The Council helped establish German-owned workshops, which employed Jews, and those fortunate enough to get positions in these enterprises were temporarily exempt from deportation to labor camps. The largest of these companies was Rosner Fabrik, which produced uniforms and goods for the German army. Begun as a shop with 12 stitchers, it grew into a factory complex with 3,000 workers. Unlike the typical German overseer, Rosner treated his employees with respect and fought to protect them. He even warned them of impending actions. Rosner Fabrik remained in operation until Rosner's arrest and execution in January 1944.

Sewing workshop in the Sosnowiec Ghetto. Sosnowiec, the neighboring town to Będzin, was also an "open" ghetto.
– United States Holocaust Memorial Museum

In Będzin, the Jewish Council formed local Zionist youth organizations and developed small agricultural plots on the outskirts of town. They allocated a 100-acre plot to a Zionist youth group known as the "Farma," which became a focus of youth activity. Following mass deportations of Będzin Jews to Auschwitz, a youth movement, under the leadership of activist Zvi Dunski, began urging fellow Jews not to report for the deportations. Eventually, the "Farma" became the headquarters of the Jewish underground and was the site of clandestine meetings with Mordechai Anielewicz, Arie Wilner and other leaders of the Jewish Fighting Organization in the Warsaw Ghetto. – United States Holocaust Memorial Museum

Street scene with Jewish police (wearing white armbands) in the Będzin Ghetto. – United States Holocaust Memorial Museum

Overview of the I. G. Farben synthetic rubber (Buna Werke), petroleum plant and other factories, circa 1942. The Farben plant opened in Monowitz in May 1942 to take advantage of cheap labor at the nearby Auschwitz concentration camps. The Monowitz subcamp was known as Bunalager (Buna Camp) until November 1943, when it became KZ Auschwitz III with its own administrative headquarters. The Buna plant attracted the attention of the Allies, and there were several bombing raids on the factories. Life expectancy for workers at the plant was extremely poor, with about 25,000 fatalities by 1945. – O. Ang, German Federal Archives

CHAPTER X

BUNA

We were transported by train to Buna, an enormous camp with many subcamps, about thirty miles from Krakow. Buna, so named in 1942, was also known as Auschwitz III / Monowitz, but prisoners here had a higher survival rate than the other Auschwitz camps. They were kept alive because they were needed as workers. Like Auschwitz I, the grounds were surprisingly clean in spite of the huge numbers of inmates. The prisoners, maybe ten thousand in all, were of many nationalities—Jews, Germans, Gypsies, Russians. I was assigned to the Buna Werke, a chemical factory owned by I. G. Farben, in one of Europe's largest industrial complexes. It also contained Krupp, the electric works, and Siemens/Telefunken. I worked at the latter for a time, and years later I received restitution. Some of the work was terrible, but life in the barracks was relaxed to a degree I had not known.

The day we arrived we were taken into the yard and harassed quite a bit. We stood outside for several hours, during which time some boys were beaten, and others were taken away without ever going into the barracks. Finally, about a hundred of us boys and a few men were assigned to Block 51, which turned out to be one of the best barracks in the whole camp.

I was in a triple bunk, and there was a gentleman, about forty-six, and his son just below me. The man's name was Mordechai. He told me he had a beautiful family back in Warsaw—a wife, five daughters and two sons. He didn't say what had become of his wife and daughters. I assumed the worst.

Mordechai was the most learned man I had ever met. He remembered the Talmud[1] and memorized the Torah, and he was always learning. At one time he had a tefillin and a prayer book with him. I loved being with him because I felt that I was part of his family, too. It was a sad day when he was sent to the gas chamber and his son was sent away to another camp.

We had a German kapo who was a political prisoner, guilty of no more than a minor crime. Like other political kapos, he wore a green triangle, but he wasn't like the others. For all my years in the camps, this man was the first real human being among the enemy. And he told us, "Look, pretty soon the war will be over." There was a feeling in the camp that things would be better, that the war really would be over.

When I arrived here, I needed a wooden shoe and he was in charge of the warehouse where they distributed shoes and clothing. He said, "Look, you don't want to wear those clunky wooden shoes," and he gave me a pair of leather boots. The right and left boot were different sizes, but this was the first time I had leather boots. What a relief to have some real work boots! His office was in the barracks and sometimes I worked as his office boy, or busboy. He talked to me like I was a young teenager, and I went along with it. I was short and skinny, but with the extra food I'd eaten in Będzin, I looked better than I had in some time. After working with this kapo for awhile, I started making the rounds of the camp with him, like a father and son. I can actually say we became friends.

In the barrack, we were not watched by the Gestapo or prison guards, so we could cook, mingle, talk, sing—and we did it all. Before I had my work assignment at Buna Werke, I hung around the barrack like an ordinary teenager on an ordinary day. For the guards' amusement, we often had to do something crazy. For example, one morning after roll call, we were forced to go marching and singing with the band.

At Buna, there were many storage barracks filled with various supplies. There were barracks for shoes, clothing, medical supplies, food, everything. Our kapo dreamed up ideas of things to do to fill the day, and one of them was to steal from the supply barracks. One day when many of the barracks were unguarded, he said, "Look, go in and bring out some heavy blankets."

So I slipped in and carried them out, five from this barrack, six from that one, and we brought them back to Block 51. He traded the blankets for other things or gave them away.

Shoes taken from prisoners upon arrival fill one of many storage supply barracks at Auschwitz. – Yad Vashem Archives

One day he told me to search for valuables, so I looked under blankets and cots, checked nooks and crannies. Some of the inmates had small knives, little silver things like cigarette lighters, and we piled up all kinds of stuff. I had no choice in the matter—he was my kapo, my boss, and he ordered me to do it. He had me take out everyone's wooden shoes and throw them out and he replaced them with leather shoes taken from the supply barracks. He said he was going to make Block 51 the best in the camp with the best stuff. Unfortunately, the story does not end well.

Many weeks passed, and we were having a hell of a time in Buna. One day, I was busy pilfering things with the kapo, when there was a surprise inspection in the barracks. Four or five jeeps filled with SS men swept in to inspect the camp and headed for the lazarett. The Nazis were big on numbers. How many people were sick? How many dead? One guy saw me walking into a barrack with the kapo, my arms full of blankets, and he called out, *"Machst du hier?* What are you doing here?" He sent me back to Block 51 and then had a private conversation with the kapo, which went on and on. I stood there trembling in my shoes.

Finally the SS man came to fetch me and said, "You damned Jew! You are stealing from the camp and you must be punished for this." He took out a piece of paper, copied down the number on my arm and pinned it to my shirt, a real bull's eye on my chest, where everyone could see it. "Wear it," he ordered.

In the early morning, during roll call, my number was called over the loudspeaker. "The prisoner with this number should report to…" Imagine this! My God, I was scared to death. I informed the kapo and said I didn't want to go. I took a chance, I didn't care. I knew harm would come to me if I went. Inmates were punished by shootings and hangings, we knew this. Several times they called my number over the microphone, telling me to report to this particular place, but I didn't go. When everybody went to work, I hid in the barrack, alone and afraid. This went on for three or four days. By then, I had taken the number from my chest, ripped it up and hid the pieces, but I was no longer safe in Block 51.

I looked around and noticed there was a special group of two hundred or so young boys in a different block and I thought my best chance was to hide among them. The next morning, I stood with them for roll call, shaking with fright. The Gestapo knew I was missing, but they were looking in Block 51. After several days, they stopped calling my number. Had I been caught, I'm certain I would have been punished severely. In Buna, most punishment was meted out at the gallows. Hanging was the preferred method of extermination. If killing was not executed by

hanging, then it was done by shooting. Anyway, thank God I took a chance. It also helped that the camp was so huge—so many thousands of people.

I stayed among the kids for a long time, five weeks or so. The number of our group was one hundred sixty-eight—I recall it even today—and we had *aussenkommando*—work assignments outside the camp. One night around sunset, when it was already a little dark, we saw trains filled with soldiers passing as we walked back to camp after finishing our day's work in a factory, where we had been cleaning up containers. I thought they were coming from the Russian Front and going back to Germany. We were ordered to sing as we walked. We crossed the train tracks, then something really terrible happened.

A crazy soldier on the slow-moving train observed us and took out his machine gun. He began spraying us with bullets, killing about fifteen boys and wounding many more, including me. A bullet went right through my left arm! I was a bloody mess, stunned and dizzy. How I got back to camp I'll never know. I remember being taken to the lazarett, where I lay on a bed in pain for about three weeks. I also remember being terribly hungry for days at a time. It was a strange time and I just lay on the bed for a very long

Jewish forced laborers from Auschwitz III at work building the Buna plant for I.G. Farben, circa 1943. Farben was a conglomerate of eight leading German chemical manufacturers, including Bayer, Hoechst and BASF, which at the time were the largest chemical firms in existence.

Holocaust Education & Archive Research Team

time, until I was well enough to return to work. It's remarkable that they allowed me to heal and didn't put me down like a wounded animal. But they didn't. Once again, I escaped certain death.

With this group of kids, there were times when we were between assignments and there was no work. So, to kill time, we were taken to an open field and ordered to load fifty- to one hundred-pound stones into a wagon and then unload them, for no purpose. It was just to keep us occupied. The men always had work, but not the kids, and I was passing for a kid. This went on for a few days.

One morning on the way to the field of stones, I could hear two German officers talking. One said, *"Wie viel Juden mussen wir heute tot schlagen?* How many Jews do we have to kill today?" I couldn't believe what I was hearing. Then, the reply: *"Zehn Juden."* Ten! Imagine how I felt. I knew ten of us would be sacrificed that day. The first guy followed up by asking, *"Waarum machen wir es nicht zwanzig?* Why don't we make it twenty?"

They were debating numbers! This was a horrible, sickening situation. We were going to work knowing that some of us would not be coming back. Anyway, our work assignment was worse than usual that day, and I figured this was how they would make their quota. They put a ladder in the field, then ordered us to climb it while carrying stones. Then we had to carry them down again—up and down, up and down—while one of the men whipped us over the head, the feet, the hands, the eyes. This is how the boys fell. Some couldn't make it up anymore, so they lay on the ground, doomed. Every day there were fewer and fewer of us, every day more kids gone.

One evening when we returned from this craziness, tired and hungry, they decided our group would be punished because one boy took a few minute's rest while working. The punishment would be humiliation. As usual, we were fed soup about an hour after returning from our work. But, while we often drank our soup straight from our bowls, rarely with the luxury of a spoon, this day they made us eat the soup on our elbows and knees, like dogs. We were starving too much to let pride get in the way.

On one very cold evening in late December, the soup was taking longer than usual, so I drifted back to the barracks. Snow was on the ground and it was around sunset; it looked beautiful. I carried a small knife a friend had given me before he was taken to the gas chambers, a

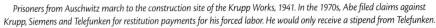

Prisoners from Auschwitz march to the construction site of the Krupp Works, 1941. In the 1970s, Abe filed claims against Krupp, Siemens and Telefunken for restitution payments for his forced labor. He would only receive a stipend from Telefunken.

Yad Vashem Archives

tiny, beautiful, antique knife. I was so hungry, I swapped the knife with another boy for a piece of bread. Unfortunately, the kapo in charge, a German Jew named Paul, was watching and saw the transaction.

Some of the German Jews, I'm ashamed to say, were as brutal as the SS. They got their orders from the SS, which they had to follow, but they could have done things to help us not suffer so badly. Instead they did everything they were told, and sometimes more. For their barbarity they got better rations, better clothes, more privileges.

Paul asked me, "What kind of deal did you make?" I said nothing. "Where did you get that bread?" I mumbled something and handed him the bread. He said, "You broke the law."

Suddenly he went wild and grabbed me with both hands. He was very strong and I weighed about a hundred pounds, so I couldn't fight back. In the middle of the barracks was a freestanding stove, and it was very hot. By this time, everybody was watching, and I was wailing and yelling. Paul put me on the stove and held me there for about a minute, burning my whole behind from below my waist all the way down my butt. He then threw me on the floor and left.

I staggered back to the barrack, lay down on my bunk and wept. Everyone was upset by the brutality. As darkness fell, I couldn't sleep from the pain; blisters erupted all across my buttocks. I still hadn't eaten. I just lay on my belly. Nobody came in to see me. The two boys lying below me asked what they could do, but they could only sympathize. I fell asleep for an hour in the dark and cold, then somebody woke me up. I couldn't understand what was happening. I thought I was going to be taken away forever. But this guy came back with a doctor and asked, "*Ich hab' viel schmerzen?* How do you feel?" I told him that I was in awful pain. It was the heartless Paul himself, perhaps in a moment of regret. I was surprised he had called in a doctor.

I knew the doctor. He was an inmate who worked in the hospital in the rear of the camp. He drained my blisters while I screamed. I prayed to God, suggesting maybe it would be better that I die. It was a new low point in my life. The doctor put fresh bandages on my buttocks and left. I guess I must have wanted to live because I asked the boy in the bunk below to get me some soup and bread. And so he did. This was how life went. I lay on my belly every day for two or three weeks, useless to the Germans now, and I worried constantly that somebody would come and take me to the death house. I was exhausted from the pain and constant hunger.

Eventually, I began to heal. And the moment they saw that I was beginning to recover, they rushed me back to work. We were doing real work again. For a time we worked in one of the ammunition factories. Using a big, eight-pound electric drill, I'd make holes in artillery shells, in the metal casing, which was very hard work. From there we were sent to different factories to do a variety of jobs.

One day we returned from work, and there was something new planned for us. As we waited in roll call before supper, the SS men took ten boys out of the line and led them to a big washroom. One of the boys was the friend who had brought me food when I was sick. They turned up the water in the washroom to make a pool in the long sink. The boys were forced to stand alongside the sinks. The SS men then held their faces down in the pool of water until they drowned. We had to take them away. Every day they found new ways to fulfill their kill quota—new ways to get rid of us.

Buna was a very cruel place. I witnessed a scene where a group of women were working in the fields not far from us, picking potatoes. As usual, we were hungry so we thought we could make a connection to get them to bring some potatoes back. One of the boys walked very close to them and stole a few potatoes. The SS saw this and ordered immediate punishment for our entire column. When we returned to the scene of the crime the next day, he ordered the women, "Dig!," so they began digging large holes. There were fifteen to twenty women of all ages. Half were ordered to get into the holes, their graves, and the other half had to bury them alive. We were forced to witness this. This was our punishment.

Death March to Gleiwitz

It was mid-December and nearly every day now we heard the sound of planes flying overhead. We weren't sure where it was coming from, but we thought Krakow was under siege. Something was going on. Maybe it was the Russians, Americans or British. Then one day in early January, the bombing and artillery came raining into the camp. The barrage lasted for two or three days, but miraculously, not one shell hit the barracks. Some people say that the camp was hit accidentally, but to me it felt like the Allies or Russians were being precise with their bombs, missing the barracks deliberately, perhaps trying to scare the Germans into evacuating. The Nazis knew the Russians were only a few miles away, and they were afraid of getting caught. When the bombing stopped, the order to "evacuate camp" came over the loudspeakers at four o'clock that afternoon. All inmates were told to leave everything behind and line up in front of the barracks immediately, five people deep. Many of us grabbed blankets from our bunks or stuffed paper inside our shirts. We also stuffed a few little things in paper bags and pockets and waited outside on this dry, extremely cold night.

Even now, while we hoped we would be liberated, we believed that, in reality, we would end up like everyone else—dead. So many days we had lost hope, and other days we believed again. I was so strong in my faith that I never really lost hope. Looking back, I don't how I did it. Maybe some miracle was going to happen. It was extremely cold and dark around 5 PM, and the Germans began counting everyone in line—by nationality, gender, prisoner rank. There were about ten thousand häftling in the Buna camp, sixty thousand in the entire complex. Taking inventory took a long time. Suddenly, the evacuation plan was canceled, but we did not return to our barracks. Only after standing outside in the cold for many more hours were we told to report back to the barrack. It was a crazy thing.

The next day, a Sunday, we had no work and we sat in the barrack waiting for something to happen. At 9 AM sirens began blaring, one after the other, for more than an hour, followed by warnings over the loudspeaker, "Stay in the barracks." Ten minutes later we went out for roll call and, at that moment, hundreds of Russian planes flew over—so low we could see their markings. Buna was one of the largest industrial

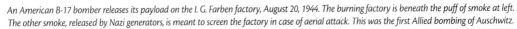

An American B-17 bomber releases its payload on the I. G. Farben factory, August 20, 1944. The burning factory is beneath the puff of smoke at left. The other smoke, released by Nazi generators, is meant to screen the factory in case of aerial attack. This was the first Allied bombing of Auschwitz.

National Archives, College Park, MD

areas around, with more than fifty factories. The Russians dropped bombs, one after the other, on the industrial park. Tons of bombs fell from the skies as we looked up in astonishment. The industrial park was a mass of ruin, so completely destroyed. The camp itself was not touched.

It was early January 1945. On this day there was to be a grand opening of the industrial park. A special celebration had been planned, and the high commanders from the district were invited. Now there was nothing left but fire and ruin. The Russians came so close we could almost have grabbed the shells. When the bombing stopped, we lined up in columns, miles and miles of columns stretching as far as the eye could see. It was an incredible sight—an impressive display of Nazi order—to be standing there ready to go. Now it really was time to evacuate.

A tall, skinny SS guy approached me, saying, "You're going to have to carry all my belongings." His belongings! As we started out walking, I was bent over with the weight of it. After a couple of miles, my God, I couldn't breathe, I couldn't walk. Every column had three or four SS men alongside it, shooting in the air to keep us going.

It was like a cowboy movie. They drove us like steer in a cattle drive, and they just kept driving and driving. Eventually the darkness fell; it was a beautiful night, but very cold. The snow was deep that winter and we were quickly exhausted. I knew I couldn't go on with my burden, so under cover of night, I quietly threw the bundle in the canal, muttering to myself, whatever happens, I cannot take it. I cannot carry this load. The next morning I walked very fast, until I got far away from the SS man. He never found his mule. God had given me another miracle.

This journey was truly a march of death. Those who stumbled and fell by the wayside were shot. We walked over dead bodies every few yards, people who just couldn't go any further. It was a painful experience. So many thousands killed, massacred. After walking about 30 miles, and with dawn breaking in the sky behind us, we came upon the outskirts of another large city, Gleiwitz, where I had worked before. We stopped at a vacant brick-making factory alongside a railroad depot. Inside the factory were large wooden shelves for piling bricks and we lay down on the shelves, packed together like sardines, hungry

"Evacuation," by Naomi Judkowski, 1945. The text reads, "We were sent out of Oświęcim on 18/1/45, in the direction of Wroclaw. Whoever failed to keep up was shot along the way." Watercolor is from Judkowski's album, "The Oświęcim Death Camp," used as testimony in the Eichmann trial.

"A store of 'human fuel,' handily by the ovens. The shed was full of bodies piled up to the ceiling. When the doors were opened, some cadavers tumbled out." – Photographer with the liberating Soviet army

"Frenchwomen on their way to freedom. They have shed their prison uniforms and put on clothes taken from burning magazines (sheds)." – Photographer with the liberating Soviet army

and shivering in our pajamas. We later learned that more than fifty thousand häftlings made the march, and many thousands died along the way.[2] It was a miracle that any of us survived. We waited all day without food and thought they were going to finish us off by starving us. But around six o'clock, we were transferred to a cattle train, and a man came in with big containers. Soup!

The train was so packed you couldn't slip a needle in it. The top of my car was completely open, so I could actually jump off and run, and I thought about it, but where could I go? I feared I would be shot. Everywhere we looked there were Gestapo, thousands of them. I was afraid, really. We rode only at night; the trains stood still in

the daytime. You could see the planes flying over. The Nazis were afraid we'd be bombed if their enemy saw a moving train.

Once again I survived, probably because I was in an open-air car; many others were closed in. We rode for six or seven nights, traveling as far as the Czech border, then zigzagging back. We were given soup once a day, which still left us hungry. They no longer killed us in gas chambers or by beatings. Instead, we merely died of hunger and exhaustion and were disposed of en route to nowhere. They weren't keeping us alive out of kindness—they still needed workers, and if we could survive a death march, we were fit to work.

Finally, we arrived at Concentration Camp Dora. It was late January 1945.

A fresh trail in the snow on Main Street in Birkenau, mid-January, 1945. The photo caption reads, "The trail of evacuation, marked by bodies every few steps. Those who fell were killed on the spot." The photographs on this page are stills taken from a film by Henryk Makarewicz, cameraman in the Polish Berling Army, which entered the Auschwitz camps with the liberating Soviet Red Army only a day or two after the Death March set out.

United States Holocaust Memorial Museum

Buna Monowitz (Auschwitz III)

Buna Monowitz was a corporate camp established in October of 1942 to satisfy the slave-labor requirements of the Buna synthetic rubber factory, Buna Werke, which was run by the German corporation I. G. Farben. The camp was set up around the Polish town of Monowice, not far from the Auschwitz I main camp. Between 1942 and 1945, approximately 10,000 Jewish inmates were brought to Monowitz from Auschwitz I.

I. G. Farben paid the SS for the use of its slaves. Farben also agreed to pay several sick days for infirm prisoners. This prompted the SS to establish a practice whereby only 5% of the prisoner population could be absent due to illness at any time. Thus, to prevent an excess of infirm prisoners, the SS routinely sent them to a gas chamber at Birkenau, or relied on physicians to cull the population through "scientific" experimentation. Ultimately, most prisoners at Buna would die of starvation, disease, daily beatings at the work site, or execution. Many would perish along the road to Gleiwitz during the "death march" evacuation in January 1945. [Wollheim Memorial]

Ukranian forced laborer welding at I. G. Farben in Monowitz.
– O. Ang, German Federal Archives

Construction of the Krupp factory near Auschwitz by forced laborers. – Yad Vashem

Bombing Buna

On January 12, 1945, the Soviet Army began the massive Vistula-Oder Offensive, one of its most successful military operations, striking deep inside occupied Poland. Red Army planes struck the Buna Werke on January 16 and left the facility scarred, but intact. As Abe tells it, the attack caused the SS to gather prisoners for a massive evacuation of the entire Auschwitz system.

On January 17th, the order was given to begin evacuation of the Buna facility. Over the next four days, 56,000 prisoners from the three camps and several subcamps began marching westward. These death marches proved to be as brutal as the camps. They marched in heavily guarded columns of about 1,000,

Original caption reads: "Kanada burns. Before leaving, the Germans set fire to magazines and piles of prisoner's clothing." Photo is taken from a film by Henryk Makarewicz immediately after the Red Army liberated Auschwitz in mid-January 1945.
–United States Holocaust Memorial Museum

while SS guards beat or shot any prisoner who lagged behind or tried to escape. The result was nearly 3,000 corpses were left along the trail in Upper Silesia. Ultimately, 35,000 to 40,000 prisoners reached Gleiwitz, where they were crammed onto rail cars and transported to camps deeper within the Reich. [Wollheim Memorial]

This Nazi propaganda photograph depicts prisoners laboring in a relatively calm, clean setting. It is from a collection of still color photographs taken by filmmaker First Lieutenant Walter Frentz, a permanent attache to the Fuehrer's headquarters. Frentz, who was given special film assignments, was asked to prepare a movie about the V-1 missile for use in newsreels. The film describes production in the missile factory and labor supplied by the Dora-Mittelbau camp in early July 1944. – Yad Vashem Archives

Chapter XI

Dora and Ellrich

When we stumbled out of the railroad cars, I was so weak I thought the day had finally arrived when I would die. KZ Dora was located in Nordhausen, East Germany in the mountains. I had no strength to climb a mountain, so I grabbed onto a friend and we started walking. We held hands and climbed up little by little. The guards climbed with us until, eventually, we came to the barracks. I remember being very cold, nearly freezing. The barracks were located in the woods, up on the hills. It was a sprawling area, like a city. I remember that one of the barracks in a beautiful area had a sign in front reading, *Internment Wehrmacht*. This was reserved for SS or soldiers who had transgressed in some way, like not obeying orders. Here they would be punished and rehabilitated. Imagine, a reform school for naughty Nazis!

Our barrack was one huge, open room and three hundred boys settled in. There was electricity but no heat, no beds, nothing. But as we looked out, we saw far below us a barrack with a kitchen. We always sniffed the air to locate the kitchen—it was the first thing we did.

We were painfully hungry and thirsty, but there was no food. There was plenty of water however. The Germans opened the water taps—fifteen of them—why so many, I don't know. Everyone was so desperate to get water, they knocked each other down, then the fighting started. I didn't even try. An hour later some Gypsies arrived—the Germans had assigned them as kapos to watch this particular barrack, and they were a murderous group. They went after us right away, for no reason, with rubber truncheons, sticks and whips, beating us over our heads, feet and bellies.

We had formed a line for soup when, suddenly, those who drank the water began to wail and buckle over in pain, suffering from diarrhea. Soon they just dropped dead. Like flies coming down from the trees in summer, they dropped one after another. We believed that the water had been treated with chemicals, which would explain why it was so plentiful and why we were encouraged to drink so much. I watched this from my place in line, in awe. Finally, I got a quart of warm soup, the best medicine in the world. Having grown callous, I took advantage of so many people dying; there was enough soup now for second helpings.

When things quieted down, those of us still alive huddled down on the barrack floor to sleep. I began to feel alive again. The next night was even better; we had bunks. But nothing could protect us from the cold. It was late January, the barracks were open to the elements and the cold rattled our bones. Here in the mountains, there were no factories to labor in, so we were organized into columns and led into the woods by SS guards. We were going lumberjacking. Using a two-man saw, I worked with another boy cutting down trees, piling up wood and picking up debris. It was hard work and we were watched every second. This went on until mid-February.

Once a week the SS doctor would visit the barracks at Dora, and we were told to stand outside naked upon his arrival. He would then conduct an inspection, deciding who was fit to work or die. Those not working were labeled musselman; this included people with swollen legs or gray hair. Before being taken away the doctor asked them if they would like to go to America. In this way, in this place, high in the mountains surrounded with beautiful alpine scenery, I saw hundreds of prisoners taken out and murdered.

One day we were asked a strange question over the loudspeaker: "Do you boys want to go home?" We didn't understand what it meant, so we stood there mute and puzzled. It was a

A look inside the barracks at Dora just after Liberation, April 1945.
– Yad Vashem Archvies, courtesy of Andrea Avrutis

trap—we knew we couldn't go home. We didn't have any home, there was no such thing. Then the kapo came in and asked again. We were so certain that this was another sick trick—a new way to kill—not one person volunteered.

Another German arrived. "Tonight we need fifty boys," he said, as he looked around and chose the ones he wanted. Next thing I knew I was in a covered truck headed for camp Ellrich, a subcamp of Dora. We knew the end of the war was coming—the camps were running low on supplies and our assigned work did not seem to need doing. It was clear why we were moving so much and doing nothing—the Nazis were afraid of being caught between the Allies and the Russians. In some places they may have needed people to work. But not in Ellrich. Not now.

Stacks of wood, harvested by inmates and used for fuel or construction, litter the grounds around the barracks at KZ Dora, 1945.

– Ghetto Fighters House Archives

KZ Ellrich and the Death Train

Ellrich was a finishing camp in its most literal sense, a death camp, but there were no gas chambers; other methods served just fine. One day, with thousands of people working in the fields, a pack of large German Shepherds were brought in and ordered to attack and kill. Gallows were built and put into use. People were shot randomly. They were killing everybody. It was a horrific scene.

A sense of confusion fell over everything, beginning with the daily attacks by Russian planes. When the planes swooped down and the sirens screamed, prisoners ran from the barracks to the safety of the fields. On one such day, in a shameless act of survival, I took advantage of this chaos to raid the Yugoslavian prisoner-of-war barrack. With a friend, I boldly walked into the barrack and rifled through their fat, green duffle bags, bulging with food. We rustled several large loaves of bread as well as marmalade, cigarettes and bags of crackers. The SS couldn't see us; I wasn't afraid. There was no longer any such thing as fear of stealing. And I wasn't afraid of the shrapnel flying around me. I saw this as an opportunity! We took the food back to the field and divided it up among our group. Every day of our lives we took a chance—and this was a very good day, under the cover of the bombs.

We were here at Ellrich for most of February and March—cleaning sewers, doing brick work, whatever came up. The sun gave us some beautiful days, and we felt time passing, but we had no knowledge of the outside beyond our boundaries. We were alive because they needed us for work, not now but in the future—the Nazis still planned on having a future.

I also remember that in Ellrich there were four or five barracks where they held women from Auschwitz who had been the subjects of experiments. The Nazis must have had to transfer them here. We knew that Auschwitz had been liberated shortly after we left Buna. The Russians were so close, we could almost smell them, and we still held out hope they would sweep in and liberate us. Neither the Americans nor the British seemed to be around. Meanwhile, people were

being lined up, shot and dumped into ditches. It was the end.

Then, one cold morning toward the end of March, they came to our barrack. We were packed into trucks and driven about five miles to the open fields. What now? We were taken out of the truck and left standing for four or five hours. We watched column after column of new prisoners being marched to Ellrich, SS guards beating and shooting them along the way. What a sight to see! What were they going to do with us? This plan got off to a confusing start, and we never knew what the plan was. Finally, they put us back in the trucks, and we drove to a nearby railroad station where we were packed into boxcars, about fifty to a car, and again waited endlessly for something to happen. Most were open cars, very cold, and we were packed so tight we couldn't breathe. I fought with some other guys as I made my way to the edge of the boxcar—it was fresh air or die. We knew about death marches, but this was something new—a death ride.

Strangely, for better or worse, I felt this would be the last train ride. We traveled for eight or nine days, maybe more, without food or bathrooms. Whoever had to go did so in the boxcar; it was terrible. We were lower than animals. Many of the boys dropped and never got back up. As usual, we traveled at night and went nowhere during the day, lingering in one city or another. We zigzagged across Germany, into Czechoslovakia, into Austria, back into Germany, a crazy trip without beginning or end; it made us scream inside.

The Germans had a problem—they didn't know where to hide us anymore. In Vienna, I recall seeing the mighty Nazi war machine in a frenzy—tanks, artillery, wounded soldiers, Gestapo, Wehrmacht—moving back and forth on the rails. We didn't care about the war anymore, we could only think about water. I was so thirsty my stomach ached and I couldn't talk. My only hope was to grab some snow, which rose in dirty piles, but it was completely out of reach. So I devised a foolish but effective plan. When we started rolling, I ripped off my undershirt and rolled it into a rope, tied one of my wooden shoes to the end, lowered it and scooped up some white stuff, which I sucked down like ice cream. Wherever we traveled, I got my snow, unfortunately mixed with locomotive oil from the tracks. I feared I was poisoning myself but it seemed a sweeter death than dying of thirst.

One day we stopped in Leipzig, in East Germany, detained under the watchful eye of the Gestapo. We couldn't make sense of the scene. People were going back and forth as if doing important business, the loudspeakers were shouting, and the German Red Cross arrived with hot soup. Food at last! I could hear the conversation when the SS intercepted the Red Cross workers. *"Das ist ein vernichtung transport und das Essen werd nicht gegeben.* This transport needs to be liquidated and will not be given any food." Our hearts dropped as we watched the food disappear. When darkness fell, the train moved on.

On the ninth day, ordinary policemen in brown uniforms approached, not SS or Gestapo, and they passed out slices of bread. After nine days of not eating, it was a miracle. But it was short lived. If you take a small slice of bread and toss it into a pack of wild animals, it quickly turns to crumbs. Everyone in the boxcar was so hungry, we fought until we were left with

nothing. Imagine this scene! The big men fell, there were dead bodies so high in the car, and you were walking over them. And the few of the living that were left were fighting over a piece of bread! It was an unbelievable scene to see. People fought like wild animals until the bread was just crumbs. After nine days of no food, this is what we had come to—a scene out of the jungle.

Our journey was not yet over. We traveled another day or two until we came into Bergen-Belsen, about 25 miles from Hannover. We stood in the boxcars nearly all day. I believe that three quarters of the prisoners on that train were already dead, and that the kapo assigned to our car had been instructed to kill as many of us as possible. Without mercy he began beating us—another nightmare. By dawn he had killed seven or eight boys in the car.

We traveled again, for another day or two, going back and forth. Finally, we came back to Bergen-Belsen. The kapo had disappeared and the train just sat there. Suddenly, someone shouted, "The Germans are gone." And we saw them running away. I couldn't understand. All of the soldiers on the transport had taken off! We were alone on the train without guards.

A train carrying prisoners is liberated upon arrival at Bergen-Belsen by the Allied Army, April 1945. It was just such a train that delivered Abe.

Dora-Mittelbau

KZ Dora-Mittelbau was set up in the Harz mountains of Germany near the city of Nordhausen. It originated as a subcamp of Buchenwald but became an independent camp with 23 branches in late 1944. At Dora-Mittelbau, prisoners worked manufacturing arms in the massive armament factory that produced the V-2 rocket and other weapons. They also worked building a system of tunnels that facilitated the process. At one point, 10,000 prisoners working at the site had no living quarters, and were forced to live in the tunnels under miserable conditions. Finally, in the summer of 1944, wooden barracks were built to house a prisoner population of over 12,000.

While working on the armaments, large numbers of prisoners were arrested on charges of sabotage and many were killed during or after their interrogations. Over 200 prisoners were hanged, including some leaders of the underground resistance. The Nazi evacuation of camps Dora and Ellrich began on April 1, 1945 and the majority of prisoners (including Abe Landau) were transferred to Bergen-Belsen. Thousands were murdered en route. At one point, near the small village of Gardelegen, the SS stuffed a barn with prisoners and set it aflame; those who survived were shot attempting to escape.

- Holocaust Education & Archive Research Team

After Liberation, freight cars are brought out of one of the tunnels in the Nordhausen hills near camp Dora, where V-series rockets are produced. – Photograph by O. Ang. German Federal Archives

Prisoners from Dora-Mittelbau, Ellrich and other subcamps produced V-series rockets and "buzz bombs" in this underground factory, 1944. – Photograph by O. Ang. German Federal Archives

Ellrich

KZ Ellrich began as a subcamp of Buchenwald and was later incorporated into the Dora system. When Dora became the Mittelbau main camp, Ellrich was eventually named Mittelbau II. Forced laborers at Ellrich primarily worked building a tunnel through the relatively soft stone of the Harz Mountains.

Dora-Mittelbau prisoners, under the supervision of German technicians, attach the completed tail apparatus to the engine and body of a V-2 missile, July 1944. – Yad Vashem Archives

Ellrich was infamous for its callous SS leadership and its inadequate facilities. Built on the ruins of an abandoned gypsum factory called Juliushutte, the camp was sometimes referred to as Ellrich-Juliushutte. When the first 300 prisoners arrived at the new camp, several blocks were without roofs. Prisoners were mainly Soviet, Polish, German and French POWs, though some of the "qualified" Jews sent from Auschwitz to Dora ended up at Ellrich (such as Abe Landau). Many were young boys. Though the death rate began relatively low—only 17 recorded in the first month—prisoners perished at a rate of 500 per month by December 1944 and up to 1,000 per month by March of 1945.

A death train of prisoners arrives at Bergen-Belsen just after Liberation, April 1945. – Yad Vashem Archives, courtesy of Meira Edelstein

Chapter XII

Bergen-Belsen and Liberation

Starvation did strange things to us; we couldn't see or think right. We stood for hours, eyes peering out of faces that had, for the most part, been reduced to nothing more than skin and bones, too afraid to leave the train. Finally we opened the door, but even then we didn't go out. After three or four hours, a woman came by, a woman! It seemed like a long time since we'd seen a woman—Bergen-Belsen had about twenty-five to thirty thousand female inmates. She said, "Look! The Germans are gone already. The Germans are gone. Why don't you get out of that train?" We stood and gawked, afraid to leave. Little by little, we began to leave the cars. I was so weak I couldn't walk and kept falling down.

It was mid-April, perhaps a few days before my twenty-third birthday. At this time, armed British troops flooded into the camp on foot and in jeeps and tanks. They seemed shocked at what they were looking at and got right down to business, assessing our needs. Our transport must have stood out as an emergency, so they gave us priority, moving us to a complex of brick buildings nestled in the woods, a camp that was clean and, by my standards, gorgeous. No wonder! They were the barracks where German officers had been stationed. The bunks were made up as if the men had planned to stay there that very night.

They put me in a special barrack and tried to evaluate my situation. I couldn't talk, my throat was constricted and my stomach was squeezed shut from the oily snow. I was taken to the hospital on the campgrounds by British soldiers and diagnosed with severe malnutrition, diarrhea and other mysterious ills. A Red Cross nurse weighed me at eighty-two-and-a-half pounds, all bones. More nurses brought in some American foods, including sweets, without realizing this was foreign food to us, and it made us more ill.

I was further diagnosed with cholera, a life-threatening illness, which they treated with medications. A skin infection swelled my face like a balloon and spread over my entire body, giving me severe headaches. Finally, my teeth were declared a disaster area. I had a mouth full of rotten and broken teeth, and my gums were so swollen, the doctors decided to operate immediately. I was put to sleep and they took a chainsaw to my gums, cutting them top and bottom and removing all my teeth and roots. Now I was just one big mouth full of pain. A German dentist fitted me for false teeth after weeks of healing.

Getting my teeth fixed had made a huge difference to my health. I gained weight for the first time. Three months passed, and I now weighed ninety pounds. I still couldn't eat much—my stomach wasn't right. Then one day, while still in the hospital and improving, this strange and lovely feeling came over me. My mind and body were in a new place, and I was actually feeling good, happy in a way I hadn't been in a long time. Could it be? I had survived the nightmare. I was liberated! This was the first time I actually realized I was free.

At the same time, I was in deep despair and grieving. I had nobody in the world. No mother, father, brother or sisters. No relatives I knew of, except a long-lost cousin in Great Britain. I was an orphan with only a few friends from our last camp. The friends I'd made in other camps had disappeared into history. I began to feel the pain of loneliness for the first time.

During the war, I had to focus on survival, there was no time to think about loss. And now these other feelings began flooding over me; I was drowning. I started to have terrible nightmares about all the bad times in the camps. Night after night I couldn't sleep, and I'd cry out and pace the halls and cringe in a corner. Doctors were alarmed. I was put in the care of a British psychiatrist who asked all kinds of questions about the camps and I slowly told my story.

With each nightmare, I thought I would die. It was as if somebody had dropped a ton of coal on my chest, and it pressed deep down, crushing me, and I broke into terrible sweats. The nightmares didn't go away, so I was sent to a special treatment home in Bergen-Belsen for several months, until I felt sane enough and strong enough to go back to the barracks. The treatment was excellent.

The United Nations and the Jewish Distribution Center (JDC)[1] stepped in to help the camp with its growing population. A large number of women had been liberated from Bergen-Belsen, and hundreds of men were coming in from camps all over Germany with the intention of meeting some nice girls. Most people had lost their entire families in the war, and everyone was very alone and lonely—it was a natural thing to do, to want to meet people. The

Bergen-Belsen inmates receive medical care after Liberation.

Yad Vashem Archives, courtesy of Harold Crabtree

A prisoner enjoying canned food at Bergen-Belsen after the Liberation.

Yad Vashem Archives, courtesy of Iris and Jack Bolton

A social life grows with food, clothing and freedom at Bergen-Belsen.
– Yad Vashem Archives, courtesy of Iris and Jack Bolton

Liberated prisoners find water aplenty at Bergen-Belsen.
– Yad Vashem Archives, courtesy of Iris and Jack Bolton

UN and JDC registered everybody and assigned us to barracks and beds and gave us a few pieces of furniture. I was living with three other boys. Our ration cards were good for coffee, flour and food that we could cook up ourselves. Many people tried to finagle extra rations but it wasn't proper. They had been so hungry in the camps that they were afraid to be without food again.

One fall day I was standing in line with my card, waiting for my rations, and about fifty young women were in the same line. I noticed a woman standing just in front of me that seemed very nice, so I introduced myself and got acquainted with her. There was a spark; she was so very pretty and so nice. Her name was Freida. As it turned out, the friend who had been liberated with me—who told me stories about Warsaw, where he grew up, and the adventures he'd had there with his friends—knew Freida very well. He told me about her family. Her mother and sisters had been with her all through Auschwitz and Bergen-Belsen. But after Liberation her mother died, possibly from overeating after years of starvation. Her father had died in the camps, but her brother had survived. Freida was twenty and I was twenty-three. He had such good things to say about her, I said, "Look, I would like to meet her again."

Prisoners stand in line to receive food rations distributed by the British army. It was in this line that Abe first met Freida. The photos on this page were taken in April 1945 by Charles Curtis Mitchell, an American soldier, and donated to Yad Vashem by his daughter, Iris Bolton.

Yad Vashem Archives, courtesy of Iris and Jack Bolton

In the next few months I spent a lot of time with her and my Warsaw friend. I liked her so much I thought about marrying her, but not before we had a chance for a real future. I needed to know more about what was going on in the cities, so I said to her, "Look, I'm tired of living in the camp. I have to get out and see what there is to do, see how I can make a living." She agreed.

So I got together with four or five guys, and we set off to see the world. From Bergen-Belsen, we took the train to Hamburg, and I wore the same pajamas I'd worn in the concentration camp. The JDC tried to give us decent clothes, but I said "Not this time." I wanted to show the Germans we had survived and were free. We had no money, nothing, and we walked around Hamburg, wide-eyed at the destruction, dodging gaping holes and inspecting ruins as if it were a lost civilization. Some Germans eyed us with suspicion and fear, others offered us soup, money and conversation.

We discovered there was a Jewish Distribution Center not far from the railroad station, and we walked in off the street and found a home. The workers were German Jews and former residents of Hamburg, who had returned. They kindly gave us food and a room overnight. We returned to Bergen-Belsen with a desire to explore further. I wore some regular clothes back; I had made my case. I told Freida everything, how the city was in ruins and how strangely the Germans looked at us. Freida knew nothing of life outside the camp, and she listened intently to every word.

Two days later three of us men left for Hannover, another big city about twenty miles away, and it too was in ruins. We could see that it had been a nice city and might be again. An established Jewish Center had set up on the *Ulrichstrasse*, and workers were registering people for food and clothing. At that point, one of my friends said, "Look, why do you want to go back to Bergen-Belsen? There's nothing for you there." He was almost right, except that Freida was there. We walked the streets for a few hours, and the Germans who passed by looked us over, and we looked them over. Some shopkeepers were staring out their windows, studying us as if we were aliens. They seemed afraid of us. We were drawn to the food, so carefully laid out, a still-life painting of fruits and sausages.

In the city, I looked into a bakery window for several minutes, just staring at the wonderful breads. "My God, this is unbelievable," I said to my friends. After so many years of having nothing to eat, to see all this food was just astonishing. My stomach was still not right, but I kept staring at the bread, as if its very existence was a miracle. If it was on my table, I couldn't eat it. But I just wanted to believe in it.

Next to the bakery was a café, and beside the café was a Herren, a men's clothing store. A pregnant German woman stood outside and asked me where I had come from. I replied Bergen-Belsen. She asked if I was married or had relatives. "No, I'm on my own." She looked me over carefully. "Are you looking for a room? We

Freida, her cousin and youngest sister, Esther, pose diffidently alongside a Bergen-Belsen crematorium, 1946.

Landau Family Collection

Abe, Freida and her sisters and cousin pose at the memorial at Bergen-Belsen, erected one year after Liberation, April 15, 1946.

Landau Family Collection

Hannover, 1946, where 88 Allied bombing raids killed more than 6,000.

A street in Hannover during American occupation, 1949.

have a very nice room for rent." What? Of course I was interested. But how do you rent a room with no money? So this nice lady took us to the fifth floor and showed us a studio apartment with two beds and a kitchenette. We had to walk through her living room to get to it. "I would like to help you out as much as I can," she said. "You won't have to pay." Her name was Mrs. Terbulen, and her husband was away on business. She had a two-year-old daughter.

At this crossroads, our trio split up. One friend decided to return to Bergen-Belsen, but my other friend and I stayed for several months in the apartment. We got acquainted with the city and tried to build a life for ourselves. Mrs. Terbulen's husband never appeared, and when I asked about him, she said, "Oh, he's coming, he's coming." I didn't have a job yet, but I made some new friends and tried to live a normal life. I heard that the JDC had put together a *Hoschschule*[2], a vocational trade school, where I could learn tailoring and other skills, or take languages if I was considering immigrating to Sweden or the U.S.

It was a strange time in my life. I didn't know where to go or what to do. I walked around looking happy, but inside I was mourning. I couldn't bring my family back, and I couldn't feel at peace with myself. Some nights I cried. I began hanging around the JDC with a group of young men, and we'd have long talks about the world. One guy brought up the subject of going back to Poland, to find lost family members. I thought to myself, Look, I'm very homesick, and I have nothing to lose. My roommate didn't want to go, but the other young man did. Maybe there was

a member of my family still living in my house, I thought. Maybe I would find a relative or something. I had no money but you could hitchhike and get free rides very easily.

So we hitched a ride from Germany to Szczecin, a city in northwestern Poland. I had no passport, nothing, just a ration card with my name and some wrong dates on it. My friend wanted to go to Warsaw but I talked him into going to Kalisz and Wilczyn first, about two hundred miles away. We took a long journey by train, horse and wagon to my boyhood home.

The Russians were occupying the town, and soldiers were everywhere. It was late afternoon, the end of November, and already dark. I was growing excited and worried about seeing our house. For a moment, I imagined my mother and father still there, my father sewing, my mother cooking, everything the way it was. We approached slowly, trying not to call attention to ourselves. And there it was! My beloved home. It hadn't changed at all, except in one way. It was now occupied by Polish people. I slipped behind the house to the backyard, took out my flashlight and dug up the box my father had buried. I tucked it in my pocket.

As we were leaving to visit a neighbor, a man stepped out of our house. He spotted me and said in Polish, "I know you—you're Jacob's son. My God, I thought all the Jews were killed. And you're still here!" He recognized me from my father's store and said angrily, "They told us every Jew was killed and there were no more Jews!" He was increasingly agitated, and I asked him why he was getting so worked up over seeing a Jew. I expected he would take me in and say that it's a good thing I'm alive and offer me a meal or something. Instead he was acting like a gangster. No doubt he thought I had come back to evict him and claim the house.

We got out of there quickly and moved on to the home of a Polish family whose son was an old friend of mine from school. He recognized me right away, and his mother, Mrs. Tomazak, was very nice. She fed us and asked us to stay overnight. We accepted.

In the predawn dark, his father came into our room and said, "You know, I have to tell you something personal. There are Russian police looking for some Jews in the city. You need to leave." I began to worry because I had no papers and wondered if I could be thrown in jail. "I have a horse and wagon," he said, "and instead of your going back to Poznań on the train, I'll take you in another direction." We had no choice. We took the wagon to the train station in Konin, about 35 kilometers away, and a train to Warsaw.

We walked around Warsaw for a couple of days and went to see the ruins of the Warsaw Ghetto. In the cemetery, the ground was still fresh from the blood of the thousands who had lost their lives. Nothing had healed; everything

was still new and raw. People were crying and looking for relatives. I ran into a Polish friend who'd been in the camps with me. He had just come in from his hometown of Czestochowa, which was known as the home of the black Madonna—the Virgin Mary depicted with dark skin. He had gone back home to look for relatives, same as me, and an unusual situation developed. A large group of Polish soldiers called NAKA, like the National Guard, had just returned from Great Britain, where they'd been fighting. Many Jewish boys were waiting at the train station, unaware of the danger. The NAKA took out their machine guns and shot down forty or fifty of them—after Liberation! My friend witnessed this. Imagine after surviving the camps under the Germans, they had come home to look for relatives and were killed by the Polish army.

Now it was becoming ever more clear why we were so afraid to be here. The Poles were the biggest anti-Semites of all. We were afraid to be in Poland any longer, the country I had grown up in. We were afraid of the people. So I said to myself, Look, I've been through so much and God gave me my life back. I will not be sacrificed in Poland by a miserable bomb-throwing anti-Semite. We needed to get out of here.

Survivors of the Kielce pogrom await transfer out of Poland, 1946. A brutal pogrom took place when the local population, fearing that the few Jewish survivors would return home to recover their belongings, started a rumor that Jews had murdered Christian children and drank their blood. The rumor took hold, and in the end, forty-two Jews were murdered and hundreds of thousands more from throughout eastern Europe began emigrating.

Yad Vashem Archives

Bergen-Belsen

On April 8, 1945, around 25,000 to 30,000 prisoners arrived at Bergen-Belsen from concentration camps throughout northern Germany, swelling the population to over 60,000. When the camp was liberated on April 15, 1945 by the Allied 21st Army Group, a combined British and Canadian unit, it was rife with starvation and disease, including typhus. An estimated 50,000 Russian prisoners of war and another 50,000 inmates died there, up to 35,000 dying of typhus in the first few months of 1945.

When the British arrived, over 13,000 corpses lay around the camp unburied. The BBC's Richard Dimbleby, reported:

> Here, over an acre of ground lay dead and dying people. You could not see which was which....The living lay with their heads against the corpses and around them moved the awful, ghostly procession of emaciated, aimless people, with nothing to do and with no hope of life, unable to move out of your way, unable to look at the terrible sights around them.... Babies had been born here, tiny wizened things that could not live....A mother, driven mad, screamed at a British sentry to give her milk for her child, and thrust the tiny mite into his arms, then ran off, crying terribly. He opened the bundle and found the baby had been dead for days.

To eradicate the disease, the British burned down the camp and a new Displaced Persons center was erected nearby. At the DP, there was a rebirth of family life, with an average of 20 weddings per day. After the first few months, 2,000 children were born in the camp.

"The Beast of Belsen," Commandant Josef Kramer, is arrested by the British. He was later convicted of war crimes and hanged.

Soup aplenty outside Kitchen B, after Liberation, April 1945.

British soldiers burn the barracks to eradicate typhus.

British soldiers force female German guards to evacuate bodies after the liberation, April 1945.

Recovering women display their Auschwitz tattoos, 1945.

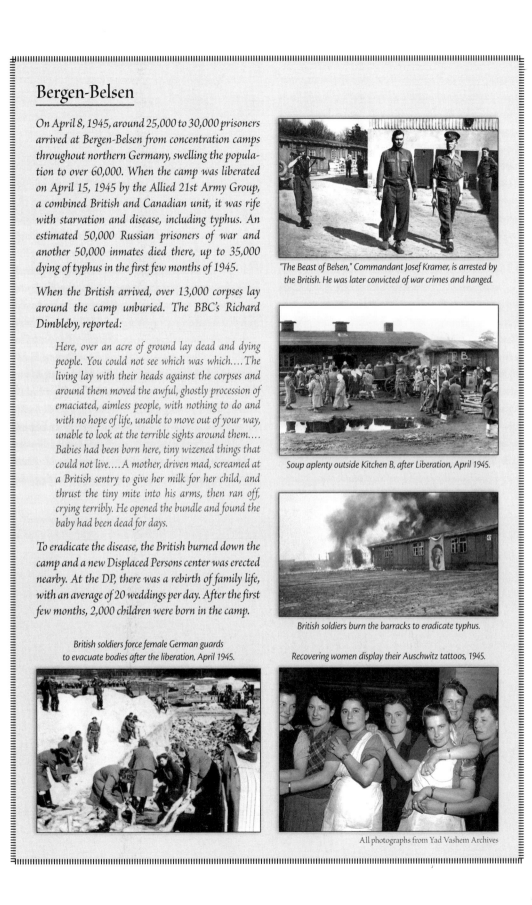

All photographs from Yad Vashem Archives

113

Abe's gang of friends—the boys he traveled with to places like Hamburg, Warsaw and Munich. Abe is at far right. – Landau Family Collection

Chapter XIII

Hannover

After five days, we returned to Hannover, where I had already established a bit of a life. It was now early 1946. On Saturdays I attended classes at the vocational school and learned my father's trade, tailoring. I also attended the German Conservatory of Music to learn to play the violin—I still have that first violin.

At this time, Hannover was occupied by the British. Twice a week I'd go to pick up my rations from the Jewish Center, and one day I met an British officer there, a major, and he asked me all kinds of questions—where I came from, how I was liberated and so on. We had many conversations and soon became very close. When he visited me, my landlady had to let him in. He apologetically trooped through her living room to get to my room. Her husband had returned in February and was a man of few words. He said nothing about his work, which made me even more curious.

The British officer and I talked about religion, about the camps, about world affairs. When he planned to go back to England on furlough for two months, he asked if he could bring anything back. I told him I had an uncle in England, a wealthy man who had lived there long before the war. I knew his city and street but not the exact street number. "If you have a chance, please look him up and let him know I survived." I expected nothing from this and said goodbye to my new friend, wondering if I would ever see him again.

Two months later there came a knock on the door. The British major stood there smiling. "Abe, I have something for you." He handed me a package from my cousin. He had written me a letter and included a tefillin and prayer book, as well as two thousand dollars in English pounds. My God, I had at least one living relative! I was so touched by this and so grateful to my friend.

Another surprise followed this one. Two cousins from Poland who were living in Hannover contacted me. We had a grand reunion and caught up on the war years. They had survived the camps and had also gone back to Poland to look for family members. In the city of Łódź, they were arrested by Russian soldiers for being involved in the black market. It was nonsense, but the Russians took their money and threw them in jail. Released a week later, they promptly returned to Hannover. The Poles and Russians were expelling the Jews—again.

After Liberation, Abe reconnected with two close cousins from̽ Wilczyn—Shmuel and Reuven Landau. - Landau Family Collection

just start crying. I had to stop asking. I knew nothing about him, I didn't even know his name.

One day Freida had an unexpected guest, a cousin from Israel who was a volunteer with the British army. He wasn't aware that Freida and I were planning on getting married, and he wanted to take her to Israel. He thought she would have a better life there, or maybe he planned on marrying her himself. I tried to make my intentions clear. "I am going to marry Freida," I declared. At first he took it as a challenge—I must have looked like a short, skinny kid from nowhere, unworthy of her. The conflict between us played out for a week, until he finally gave in. "Look," he said, "I know the way you feel. After everything you lived through, just live your life."

At that time, I didn't want to go to Israel. Things were looking up for me in Germany. I spoke perfect German, had saved some money and acquired a few possessions. I was learning tailoring and playing the violin. My contacts with German-Jewish businessmen were flourishing, and my landlady proved as generous as advertised. We could have a future here.

Every weekend after class I visited Freida at Bergen-Belsen. She was still living in the camp with the other women—about three thousand of them now, and there was plenty going on there. The Americans were big on entertainment and recreation, and Bergen-Belsen had been turned into a brightly lit city with movies, cantinas, restaurants—everything. It was a very social place, a good place for Freida to begin to heal from the war—she had experienced so much loss. If I brought up the subject of her father, she would

Abe was sent for a time to Bad Megentheim in central Germany for further recovery. Famous for its remedial mineral springs and spa gardens, Bad Megentheim had been spared Allied bombing because it was a military hospital town. At center, Abe poses with a group of fellow survivors, 1947.

Landau Family Collection

116

Freida and her cousin, a British Army volunteer, at the mass grave site in Bergen-Belsen where her mother is buried. – Landau Family Collection

A year after we met, Freida and I were married in a private ceremony. It was September 1946. First we took out our papers at the German Amt (City Hall) and later were married in a restaurant according to the Jewish tradition. Rabbi Lubinsky, a famous Polish rabbi who was liberated at Bergen-Belsen, performed the service. It was a small, intimate wedding and very nice. My two cousins, my Hannover friend, two of Freida's sisters, her cousins and close friends attended. There were hundreds of weddings in Bergen-Belsen that year, and so many rabbis who had been liberated, it was just a beautiful thing.

And then I plunged into the goose-down feather business, aided by advice from the German Jews I'd met. I would go around to different places and buy old pillows and bedding, remove the feathers and take them to an industrial cleaner. Then I'd resell them to other businesses. The demand was great. Soon I had enough money to open a store where I had my own workroom, and I applied my new tailoring skills to make beautiful new quilts and pillows. And Freida helped with the embroidery. After the war, the Germans were hungry for beautiful things, and business was so good I could produce and sell a hundred pair a week. Usually I sold them in Hamburg, a bigger city than Hannover, and I already had four hundred customers.

The war was never far away. Every now and then a peculiar thing would happen to make me think it was not yet over. One day I had to go through Munich on a business trip, which was a long, tiring trip by train. There were hundreds of Germans, Jews and other travelers on the train. Nothing was normal. Everybody was traveling, looking for something. Everything in Germany was in ruins. People seemed restless, empty, their faces vaguely absent.

A German lady sitting opposite me was wearing a Persian fur coat. I was sitting near a dozen people in the same car. One of the Jewish ladies, about forty-five, stared at the woman in the coat. "Why are you staring at me?" the woman asked in German. "I feel bad about the war, but I didn't personally do anything to you."

The Jewish woman said, "I want my coat back! That is my coat." The German woman drew the coat around her. "You must be crazy. You must be out of your mind. I bought it in a store in Germany."

"No, the coat is mine—I recognize my own coat," she yelled. When the train stopped, she started to fight the German woman, grabbing the coat. Soon the German police arrived, along with some American soldiers who were patrolling the station. "I can prove this is my coat," she

A week before being married in Hannover, September 1946.

Landau Family Collection

117

told the police. "When I left the ghetto, I sewed two diamonds in one of the shoulders and they must still be there." A policeman took the coat, ripped the shoulder seam and there were the two diamonds. The women were taken to the police station, and by the looks of it, the Jewish woman got her coat.

The Germans had possessions—furs, gold, paintings, jewelry, lots of money—they took from the Jews and lived on long after the war. People ask me even now, "Do you think every German was guilty?" I know one thing: every German who took part in the war, whether he was in the SS or the Gestapo, or in charge of a ghetto, they all knew what was happening in the camps. They knew the killing was going on. But I don't believe they revealed it to their families. Maybe they said some things after the war.

Freida had a married sister in Celle, about twenty-five miles from Bergen-Belsen. When she was pregnant and ailing, Freida went to help her out for ten days, leaving me alone. Late one Friday afternoon, I lit the candles and got comfortable listening to the radio when the mailman knocked on the door. He handed me a letter from Israel. Two of Freida's younger

sisters had settled in Israel, and they sent us a letter along with two photos of their father, which Freida had asked for. I opened the envelope and was shocked at what I saw. As I looked at the photos I was overcome with dizziness. I didn't

This portrait of Freida's father, Mordechai, shocked Abe.

believe it was possible. I kept looking at them and saying, no, it's impossible. I nearly dropped.

Freida's father was none other than Mordechai, the scholarly man with me in Block 51 at Buna. We'd had a triple bunk, and he and his son were below me. Mordechai talked about what a beautiful family he had—five daughters and two sons. In barracks such as those in Buna we had maybe a hundred and fifty inmates, and one rarely knew the name of the other, or where they came from. Everyone was occupied with his own problems. But Mordechai was different. He inspired me with his knowledge and gave me hope with his profound faith—tools that keep you alive. He was the most cultured man I had ever met.

Abe with two friends and a British soldier at the Displaced Persons camp.

Abe and his traveling buddies from Warsaw.

That I had married his daughter was just one more miracle in a life now overflowing with divine wonder. How could this be possible? Was it a dream? I cannot describe the feeling when I told Freida the story. I asked myself, was it just chance? Did God send her to me? Freida cried when she saw the pictures. Even today when I mention her father, she cries. I put one of the photos in a frame and it is still with us.

After this revelation, Freida and I became closer than ever. All we had was each other. We lived in a tiny room without much furniture and we were really very happy. We had some friends, work was going well, and I was playing the violin quite well by now. Then, Freida became pregnant. You can imagine how our happiness grew even greater. She was so beautiful, such a beautiful young lady.

But in Freida's ninth month of pregnancy, something awful happened. It was Passover, and we expected she would go into labor any time. Suddenly she looked alarmed and said to me, "I don't feel good. I don't think I'm feeling the baby." She lay down on the couch and I tried to calm her. I said, "I'm getting a taxi and we're going to the hospital." She had a German doctor, a very nice man, and we walked into his office and told him our concern. He examined her and said, "Abe, come to my office." He looked grim and I felt sick. "The situation is very bad," he said. "The baby is dead."

Abe Landau, entrepreneur, 1948.

I had to tell Freida. What else could I do? I had to tell her. I was crying—I couldn't hold back. In the hospital he induced labor; a Caesarean would have put her in danger. Freida gave birth to a little girl, stillborn—she had been dead for three or four days. And this would again throw me back deep into a dark place.

I was crying day and night. Freida, too, was sobbing all the time. We were devastated. After weeks and months, we tried to open ourselves up and live again, but something changed in us forever. I did not want to have children in Germany. How could we stay here when we had so many bad memories? How could we start a family here? It was time to go. We could go to Israel, Sweden or the United States; we could begin again.

The family portrait at left includes Freida's siblings, a cousin (seated) and her mother. Her sister Sheindel (second left) was killed with her small child at Ravensbrook concentration camp. Her youngest brother, Israel (with hat), was with Abe and Mordechai at Buna and was probably killed there with his father. Below, Abe and Freida, pregnant with their first child, enjoy an afternoon with friends in Hannover.

Landau Family Collection

Landau Family Collection

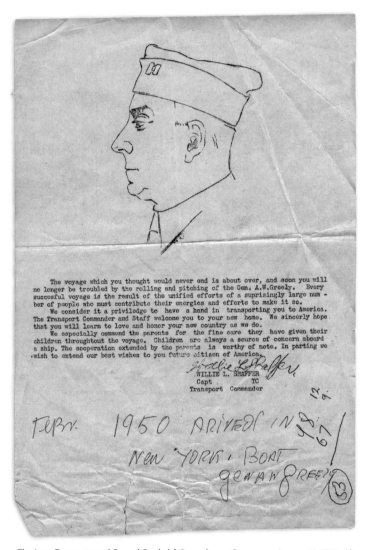

The voyage which you thought would never end is about over, and soon you will no longer be troubled by the rolling and pitching of the Gen. A.W.Greely. Every succesful voyage is the result of the unified efforts of a suprisingly large num - ber of people who must contribute their energies and efforts to make it so.

We consider it a priviledge to have a hand in transporting you to America. The Transport Commander and Staff welcome you to your new home. We sincerly hope that you will learn to love and honor your new country as we do.

We especially commend the parents for the fine care they have given their children throughout the voyage. Children are always a source of concern aboard a ship. The cooperation extended by the parents is worthy of note. In parting we wish to extend our best wishes to you future citizen of America.

WILLIE L. SHAFFER
Capt   TC
Transport Commander

FEBR.   1950 ARIVED IN
New YORK. BOAT
genAN$REE'S

The Army Transport vessel General Greely left Bremerhaven, Germany on January 18, 1950 with a passenger cargo of Displaced Persons, mostly Jews from Bergen-Belsen emigrating to the United States. This note of thanks and well-wishes was delivered to each passenger from Commander Willie Shaffer. The ship arrived at Ellis Island, February 2, 1950. – Landau Family Collection

Chapter XIV

America

We registered to go to Israel in early 1948. All you had to do was go to the Jewish Distribution Center and fill out the papers. Other places were more complicated, but eventually we made out applications for Australia, Sweden and the United States. My first choice was the U.S. but I didn't have much hope of getting a visa. Freida liked the idea of Israel because she had two sisters and a brother there. They had gone directly there after Liberation and were working in a kibbutz, as hard as they had ever worked. Israel was a poor country then, not yet established.

I also discovered that I had a close friend living there, one of six Jewish people from my hometown in Poland who had survived. I began corresponding with her husband, an entrepreneur who said he worked in the government, and he asked me to bring my sewing machines and other equipment so we could establish a little factory there. We gave this a lot of thought and after some time decided it was a good idea. It was early 1949, Israel was just established and people were being encouraged to settle. We packed all of our possessions—sewing machine, furniture, bikes, everything—in big wooden crates and were ready to go. But first I decided to check the man out, so I made the trip alone. After we met and finished talking, I realized it was a mistake. I couldn't make a living at tailoring, and he just wanted my equipment and goods.

This threw us into confusion, and we delayed doing anything. Then one afternoon we received a telegram from the Jewish Joint Distribution Committee, issuing us visas for the United States. "Looks like we are going to the United States!" We had no time to waste. We were leaving soon on a military ship out of Bremerhaven. Since we could take but few possessions, I sold almost everything we owned for peanuts and gave the rest away.

We were very happy to be leaving, for so many reasons. We hated speaking the German language every day, hated the sound of our own voices. We feared anti-Semitism would rise again. And we didn't want to be reminded of the baby, the baby who was everywhere. The Bible tells the Jews we should live according to certain laws—which animals we can eat, which unclean animals we cannot eat. There's a word for this. And the same word described my feelings about staying in Germany: It was not kosher.

But some German people, including my landlady, were wonderful. She was genuinely fond of us and did so much for us. She called me Wolfchen—a less formal version of my middle name, Wolfgang. When I asked her why she was so generous, she never had an answer. But when she knew we were leaving the country, she finally told me the truth. She said that her husband had been in the SS and confided so many terrible things, she felt she had a moral obligation to do something good. I don't know if her husband felt guilty. Our landlady was a friend of the woman across the street whose husband was also an SS officer and very open about it. He talked about

Hitler, about the Wehrmacht, about the Jews. He was very anti-Semitic.

Freida and I were on that military ship with eighteen hundred people, many of them from Bergen-Belsen, and we arrived in New York City on February 2, 1950. We spent one night in the city and were put on a bus the next day and sent to New Bedford, Massachusetts, a textile city that supposedly was a good match for my skills. But I had much bigger plans for myself—perhaps Canada and the fur trade, or a metropolis like New York City.

We were the first Jewish newcomers from Germany in New Bedford. Freida took one look around at this strange place and cried. We had never felt so alone in the world. We did not speak the language, and we were lost. Everything in America was alien to us. Some people told me that the streets were paved with gold. Well, I didn't find any gold. I felt like a beggar. I had no money, no possessions and no friends. At the same time, we couldn't go back—we had to go forward.

And so we did. Out of nothing, we built a future.

Freida (center) waits for the train that will take her and Abe to Bremerhaven where they will board the military transport ship General Greely *for passage to the United States.*

Abe's application for U. S. citizenship, 1950. Abe's application has two curious factual errors.
One of these—the date of his marriage—may be typographic because it would have been impossible for them to be married in 1936.
A more significant inaccuracy is Abe's date of birth, as he continues the deception that he is three years younger.

UNITED STATES OF AMERICA

DECLARATION OF INTENTION

(Invalid for all purposes seven years after the date hereof)

No. 11103.

TRIPLICATE
(To be given to declarant when originally issued; to be made a part of the petition for naturalization when petition is filed; and to be retained as a part of the petition in the records of the court)

COMMONWEALTH OF MASSACHUSETTS

COUNTY OF BRISTOL

In the .... SUPERIOR .... Court

of ..... BRISTOL COUNTY at NEW BEDFORD, MASS.

(1) My full, true, and correct name is ..... Abraham Landau

(2) My present place of residence is ..... 54 Russell Street, New Bedford, Bristol, Mass.

(3) My occupation is **Tailor** (4) I am **24** years old. (5) I was born on **April 25, 1925**

in **Wilezyn, Poland** (6) My personal description is as follows: Sex **male**

color **white**, complexion **medium**, color of eyes **brown**, color of hair **auburn**, height **5** feet **4** inches, weight **130** pounds,

visible distinctive marks ..... **none** ..... race **white**, present nationality **Polish**

(7) I am ..... married; the name of my wife or husband is **Fyrda**; we were married on **Sept. 17, 1936**

at **Hanover, Germany** she was born at **Lublen, Poland**

on **February 4, 1926** ; and entered the United States at **New York, N.Y.**

on **February 2, 1950** for permanent residence in the United States, and now resides at **New Bedford, Bristol, Mass.**

(8) I have **no** children; and the name, sex, date and place of birth, and present place of residence of each of said children who is living, are as follows:

(9) My last place of foreign residence was **Hanover, Germany** (10) I emigrated to the United States from

Bremanhaven, Germany (11) My lawful entry for permanent residence in the United States was

at **New York, N.Y.** under the name of ..... **Abraham Landau**

on **February 2, 1950** , on the **USAT Gen. A.W. Greely**

(12) Since my lawful entry for permanent residence I have **not** been absent from the United States, for a period or periods of 6 months or longer, as follows:

DEPARTED FROM THE UNITED STATES			RETURNED TO THE UNITED STATES		
PORT	DATE (Month, day, year)	VESSEL OR OTHER MEANS OF CONVEYANCE	PORT	DATE (Month, day, year)	VESSEL OR OTHER MEANS OF CONVEYANCE

(13) I have **not** heretofore made declaration of intention: No. ..... , on ..... at ..... (City or town)

(14) It is my intention in good faith to become a citizen of the United States and to reside permanently therein. (15) I will, before being admitted to citizenship, renounce absolutely and forever all allegiance and fidelity to any foreign prince, potentate, state, or sovereignty of whom or which at the time of admission to citizenship I may be a subject or citizen. (16) I am not an anarchist; nor a believer in the unlawful damage, injury, or destruction of property, or sabotage; nor a disbeliever in or opposed to organized government; nor a member of or affiliated with any organization or body of persons teaching disbelief in or opposition to organized government. (17) I certify that the photograph affixed to the duplicate and triplicate hereof is a likeness of me and was signed by me.
I do swear (affirm) that the statements I have made and the intentions I have expressed in this declaration of intention subscribed by me are true to the best of my knowledge and belief; SO HELP ME GOD.

Abraham Landau
(Original and true signature of declarant without abbreviation, also other name if used)

Subscribed and sworn to (affirmed) before me in the form of oath shown above in the office of the Clerk of said Court, at **New Bedford, Massachusetts,**

this **2nd** day of **August,** anno Domini 19**50**. I hereby certify that

Certification No. **A-7 408 689** from the Commissioner of Immigration and Naturalization, showing the lawful entry for permanent residence of the declarant above named on the date stated in this declaration of intention, has been received by me, and that the photograph affixed to the duplicate and triplicate hereof is a likeness of the declarant.

[SEAL]

CHARLES E. HARRINGTON,
SUPERIOR

Clerk of the ..... Asst.

By *Mollie G. Lafferty* Deputy Clerk.

Form N-315
U. S. DEPARTMENT OF JUSTICE
IMMIGRATION AND NATURALIZATION SERVICE
(Edition of 11-1-41)

e16—19119-1 U. S. GOVERNMENT PRINTING OFFICE

Landau Family Collection

Abe at work in his tailor shop at 520 Pleasant Street in New Bedford, 1967. His Auschwitz tattoo is clearly visible on his left arm. Abe was never shy about revealing this ignoble badge. – Standard-Times photograph, Spinner Collection

LANDAU THE TAILOR

by Marsha L. McCabe

When Abe Landau and his wife Freida arrived in New Bedford on February 3, 1950, they were "displaced persons" in every sense—homeless, without family or friends, and burdened by the enormous psychological weight of history. Carrying all their possessions in two boxes, they had sailed from Bremerhaven, Germany aboard the General Greeley to New York City and stayed in a shelter at the Hotel Marseilles that first night.

The next day they boarded a bus for Providence, where they transferred to get to New Bedford. They had been given seven dollars for the trip, from American Migration Services—four dollars for bus fare to Providence and three dollars to New Bedford. They arrived at the downtown bus station unceremoniously and alone, with no hopeful vision of the future.

Freida greeted the city in tears; as dreadful as Germany was, it was at least familiar, but this new place may as well have been on the moon. Abe, too, was disappointed in what he saw. He had hoped for a bigger city, perhaps New York, Chicago or Montreal, where he could learn the fur trade. Instead, the old bus depot on Middle Street was quiet and desolate—an eerie place with a few lockers, a soda fountain and a handful of tattooed Navy boys gathered near a phone booth smoking cigarettes and staring vacantly at the newcomers. But on his immigration papers Abe had identified his vocation as a "presser"; the relocation committee, affiliated with the United Jewish Appeal, determined that he would fit well in New Bedford with its textile mills and garment factories.

So here they were. The city seemed small and insular, not at all what he had in mind. Most distressing, he did not know the language, and his need to speak in the days ahead would throw him into a private hell of loneliness.

People tried to be friendly but the language barrier kept Abe a stranger. In the following days and weeks, he was so desperate to rub shoulders with his former countrymen, he would often wander over to South Water Street where the Polish vendors had set up their open markets in the streets, and he would yak away with them in Polish. Abe had a facility for language—he spoke Yiddish, Polish and German. He knew that his ability to survive thirteen concentration camps could be attributed, in part, to his skill in picking up German. Here in America, he made an effort to learn English as quickly as possible because he was so desperate to speak.

To speak.... And yet, Abe took a long time to speak publicly of those secrets he carried around with him, secrets that haunted him until the day he died.

Abe and Freida had arrived in an immigrant city—a community organized into enclaves, its people going about their business with what seemed a determined yet forlorn disposition, but there was hope. The city had some magnificent resources, just begging for people to notice. The Landaus did not see the busy port at the foot of Union Street where the ocean lapped against the wharves and the fishermen took in their catch. Nor did they see the "patrician-like houses" that Melville described in Moby-Dick or the historic streets and buildings of the old whaling port. They did not see a bustling downtown filled with clothiers and department stores that would one day be their clients. They had no sense of the community's strong family ethic, and the redoubtable moral fiber of this blue-collar town cut from the rib of America's mighty industrial machine. They did not see the beautiful seaside towns surrounding New Bedford. Nor could Abe foresee that this city would give him his voice.

In many ways, New Bedford was a good match for Abe and Freida Landau—a busy "garment city" of more than one hundred thousand people, where factories filled with thousands of sewing machines, presses, and pattern-cutters manufactured quality apparel. Abe's father had been a custom tailor in Poland and even made clothes for the czar's soldiers. In spite of his loathing for the czar, he was proud that the Russian gentry admired his fine work. As a youngster, Abe helped to pick up and deliver clothes for his father and no doubt learned a few tailoring skills himself as he observed his father at work.

After the war, Abe had actually felt he could prosper in post-war Germany, start a family, and make a life. That all changed the day that Freida delivered their first child, a stillborn girl. Devastated, Abe took it as a sign from God that they should leave Germany forever and begin a new life elsewhere. In the end, what distressed them most was hearing the guttural sounds of the German language spoken all around them. They especially loathed the sound of their own voices, for in order to get along in business, they had to speak German themselves.

Now in America, they were faced with the challenge of learning English. It would not be an easy task for them. The New Bedford Jewish community had agreed to sponsor a certain number of family units and prepared a small apartment for the new emigres. And so Abe and Freida Landau bravely began life in a new land.

The New Bedford of the 1950s was still driven by the textile industry. The big mills that once turned cotton into cloth had mostly fled South or liquidated. Many garment manufacturers from New York City and Pennsylvania were attracted to New Bedford's empty mill buildings and moved their manufacturing operations here. The city mills and factories were now making suits and pants, dresses and handbags, shoes and pajamas.

It was into such a factory that Abe Landau himself went for his first job in America. He met Jack Rosenberg who knew Meyer Levine, who owned a men's clothing store, Sydney's, and spoke some Yiddish. Through such contacts Abe got his first job in a factory where he operated a sewing machine, sewing sleeves into jackets. His new boss was upset that he had not made his quota at the end of the first day—and asked him to work faster. The Landaus had just arrived in the country on Friday and Abe had begun work on Monday. New land, new language, new job—it all happened so fast. Freida also found her way into a factory to work as a hand-stitcher. The Landaus did their

No.	*105*			WEEK ENDING	JAN 27 1951	
NAME	*Abraham Landau*					
REGULAR HOURS		*49½*		*54*	*45*	
		9½		*5*	*23*	
AMOUNT EARNED				*59*	*68*	
Less: Fed. Old Age Tax			*90*			
Less: Fed. Withholding Tax		*8*	*40*			
Less: U. S. Savings Bonds				*9*	*80*	
			50	*49*	*88*	
TOTAL DEDUCTIONS						
NET AMOUNT DUE						

Abe saved the stub from his first paycheck at the garment factory.
He worked 59 hours, making $1.10/hour. – Landau Family Collection

best but they were not happy as piece workers and did not like the noisy demands of the factory.

Nor were other aspects of American life going well for them. They must have seemed quite foreign to fellow Jews at the local synagogue for the Landaus felt they were not received warmly. When Abe learned enough English to speak to others and tried to share his story of the camps with them, "they did not want to hear." Turning away from the truth was not just a peculiarity of congregants in New Bedford at that time. America itself was not ready to hear.

The country was not in a reflective mood in the 1950s. Emerging from the Great Depression and World War II, the nation was on the move, using all of its energy to build a new prosperity. Factories hummed day and night, producing cars and prefab houses, stoves and refrigerators. Interstate highways began crisscrossing the country, paving the way for the automobile to become king of the road, while train stations fell into disuse. People left the cities for the leafy suburbs where they could have a patch of lawn, a couple of children and a mother at home to raise them. Blue-collar jobs turned into white-collar jobs, and advertising, public relations and sales were what many people did. A new middle class was being born. The country itself had turned inward, absorbed in the business of domestic production. Material goods began to fill the houses that made up the newly defined American dream.

Abe and Freida Landau were residents of a city that had precariously survived the rise and fall of the whaling industry, followed by the rise and fall of the textile industry, and was now making do with an assortment of factories that

A view from the New Bedford Hotel in downtown New Bedford, 1950. The rooftop in the foreground belongs to the bus terminal where Abe and Freida arrived that same year. The city felt cold, small and unfriendly to the Landaus, but they would eventually become rooted in its cultural fabric.

Standard-Times photograph, Spinner Collection

turned out garments, rubber tires, golf balls, automobile parts and electronic devices. It was a city where people worked with their hands, a city where fishermen braved the sea in summer and winter; a city where people punched time clocks, worked in shifts and carried lunch pails; a place where a mix of immigrants—Portuguese, French Canadian, English, Polish, and Cape Verdean— were glad to have the jobs.

Abe Landau was not cut out for doing fast-paced piecework in so-called "sweatshops." He liked to fuss and take pride in his work. He was ready to pounce on an opportunity to do business. When Abe sold his business in Germany, he had received a thousand dollars, which made up his total savings. It was this piece of cash that delivered him and Freida from the alien factory world to a little shop at 520 Pleasant Street in downtown New Bedford in 1952.

The shop, located above a store at the top of a steep set of stairs, had been the workplace of an old tailor who was ready to retire. "The business consisted of a run-down sewing machine on a torn linoleum floor," said Abe's long-time friend Ed Rudnick. But Abe and Freida fixed up the place and ultimately created a successful

business. In addition to making repairs and alterations, Abe used his talents to create custom-made suits and other garments.

In the shop, New Bedford met Abe and Abe met New Bedford. Everyone in the city who needed tailoring went to "Landau the Tailor." He could custom-make men's suits or alter women's dresses. He would mend tears, repair zippers, taper jackets—no job was too small. Abe built up

In late 1950, Abe opened his tailor shop on the second floor of the small building at right. For 35 years, Abe and Freida tailored away, making custom-made suits or doing simple alterations. The sign, "Landau Tailoring," can be seen at the far right corner of the building, 1962.

the business customer by customer, and everyone knew him as a man of good character and cheer. He would take a garment and hold it up, studying it as intently as if he were a surveying a piece of land. Besides taking the measure of a garment, he appeared to take the measure of his customer.

Freida often sat in a rocker near a back window that looked down on the street, her hands busy sewing—she never used the sewing machine. She had a beautiful face, as mysterious as the Mona Lisa. She smiled but did not speak much and many customers did not know whether she was Abe's wife or his employee.

In many ways, Abe and Freida Landau lived out the American dream. They had two children, Ann, born in 1951 and Jack, born in 1954. Eventually they were able to buy a house on Orchard Street. The children attended the city schools and had many friends. When Ann was twelve, they moved to Whittier Street in New Bedford's fancier West End, nearer the synagogue, because Freida wanted her children to have more Jewish friends. Both children went on to college.

At first, when people saw the number on Abe's arm, few dared ask questions, except for the children who were curious and unafraid. As the years passed, Abe became ever more willing to talk. The stories of the concentration camps had begun coming out and America was ready to listen. So Abe began telling his story. He explained to his customers that those with tattoos were the lucky ones, the ones deemed strong enough to do slave labor.

He found that his listeners were horrified and fascinated. He also felt he must begin speaking out publicly because the number of survivors was dwindling and eventually there would be no one left to tell what happened. This was an immense decision for Abe, a great leap into the unknown. And with that decision, Abe Landau found his voice. And in finding his voice, he became empowered as never before. His good friend Mary Schwartz encouraged him to visit the schools and speak to children. Once he agreed, she called several schools and they all welcomed him. More invitations followed. (Mary later became chairwoman of the Holocaust Committee of the New Bedford Jewish Federation.)

And so Abe got out there. He began speaking to civic groups, church groups and clubs, often

Abe displays suits and outfits he has custom designed. The photograph accompanied a feature story about Abe in the local newspaper in 1975.

129

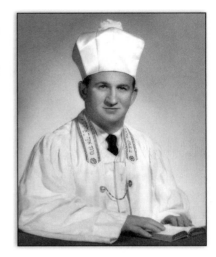

bringing his audience to tears. School children were especially moved and many wrote him heartfelt letters, telling him how his story had opened their eyes and changed their world. Abe had rapidly gone from being a private person to a public person, recognized by the city and honored by many groups. But even when film director Steven Spielberg called and asked for his testimony, Abe's heart was always home. He cherished his family life, his music and, finally, New Bedford, his adopted city by the sea.

Music was an abiding theme of Abe's life. As a boy in Poland, he aspired to become a cantor like his famed uncle Hersh Landau, who was known throughout Europe. Abe always said he owed his knowledge of Jewish music, ritual and liturgy to his father. But it was his mother's brother, the ba'al koreh who read the Torah in the synagogue in Kalisz who truly moved him.

As a youngster, his uncle took him to the synagogue. "The way the rabbi, the cantor and the ba'al koreh conducted the ceremony so moved and excited me that from then on I just had to sing," Abe once said. And so he did.

Abe never stopped singing. Even in the camps, when he was at rock bottom, he heard the melodies in his head. It's no wonder that after the war, he enrolled in the German Conservatory of Music where he studied voice and began playing the violin. Both accompanied him to America.

Ann Landau Kantor, Abe and Freida's daughter, spoke about her parents from her home in Merrick, New York where she lives with her husband, Dennis. Ann radiates warmth as she talks about her close family life.

"My father could read the entire Torah in Hebrew. He was not really accepted as a cantor in New Bedford but he was invited to sing in out-of-town synagogues. Many small congregations in New England hired him as their cantor throughout the High Holy Days—in Revere, Sharon, Framingham, and Onset. Most of these occasions were family events. Portsmouth, New Hampshire became a special place for our family because my father performed as cantor there at a particular temple over the course of six consecutive years for the high holy days.

"My father had a beautiful singing voice, full of soul. On Friday nights, he'd say 'Let's sing,' and we'd sing while I played the piano. You could hear all of Jewish history in his voice, the soulful sound of the ancients. I have never heard anyone as clear and moving as he was. He fully understood all the Hebrew texts. He felt rejected because his invitations always came from outside the area. He believed he wasn't accepted at home for what he was—Here at home he was a foreigner, he was different, but out of town he was highly esteemed. It took quite a while for him to be invited to sing in our local synagogues. And then, I think, people were astonished. They realized what a beautiful voice he had."

Abe promoted his music with a demo record that used this label. – Landau Family Collection

Abe and Freida with granddaughter Lauren Joy, daughter Ann and son-in-law Dennis, at Lauren's Bat-Mitzvah, 1992. – Landau Family Collection

Ann describes their family life and everyday routines with great appreciation. "I loved going to the tailor shop every Saturday with my mother. She did all her work by hand—she didn't use a sewing machine. She was a careful, dedicated worker, and she worked right up to the day I was born. And continued after, of course. The shop had some big accounts. The Star Store would call and say—'we've got forty pairs of pants for you to fix.' Or Wings or Swifts would call."

Ann shows her visitors a special place in her home, a room full of Abe and Freida's memorabilia. It is as if a piece of the old New Bedford tailor shop has been transplanted to Long Island. There is Abe's sewing machine, all set up and ready to go. One can imagine Abe arriving momentarily to get to the day's work. On the wall are framed photographs and newspaper articles of the couple New Bedford came to know as friends and neighbors.

Ann is grateful for all the help her parents received when they arrived in New Bedford and especially when she and Jack were born. "Max and Zadie Horenstein kind-of adopted us as their grandchildren. They knew Yiddish, which was my first language too. Max was good with his hands and made a cradle for my doll and painted it and they brought us gifts for our birthdays. Zadie always had an apron on; she baked us cakes and cookies. Other kind and wonderful families helped us too. Jack and Helene Rosenberg, Lily and Sam Feingold, Sue and Calvin Siegal. Later there was Ed Rudnick, Peter London, Jim and

Barbara Hijiya, Sean Lloyd and Betty and Paul Lestage and their family. And many, many more.

"My father was so fully informed about everything, an avid reader of books and newspapers—English, German and Jewish newspapers. He took English language classes when he first came to the U.S. That was his first goal—to learn English. He always carried a Polish-English dictionary and when he heard a word he didn't know, he would jot it down and then look it up in his dictionary that evening.

"He loved to garden and was always out there digging in the dirt. He was very romantic, always making my mother clothes and buying her lingerie. Mother never shopped. She never really wanted anything. She was happy just to be home and she loved waiting on him. She did an Eastern European style of cooking and we always had people at our Seder table. She followed a routine—she'd get up early in the morning, clean the house, cook supper for that evening, and be at work at eleven in the morning. My mother and father always worked together. I never saw a more dedicated couple.

"We were a very close family, a nucleus of four. We had adopted grandparents, but most of our larger family was gone. We talked, read, ate and sang together. We were always together. And later on, after I married Dennis and we had Lauren Joy, they found great joy in their granddaughter. And she adored them. Over the years, we traveled a well-worn path between Merrick and New Bedford. When my dad was in the nursing home

131

Granddaughter Lauren Joy lights a memorial candle during dedication of the Holocaust Memorial at New Bedford's Buttonwood Park. Rabbi Hartman is looking on. – Landau Family Collection

after a stroke, we would visit him weekly and when Lauren Joy entered the room, his eyes would light up and he would say, 'You are my whole world.' And this would be echoed by Freida."

The Landau's son, Jack, lives in Israel.

Abe and Freida's only grandchild, Lauren Joy Kantor-Finger, has fond memories of her grandparents.

"As a little girl, my grandpa Abe was always my hero, but as I grew older, he became my teacher. Now that I am an adult, he is my true inspiration in everything I do. When I speak to others about Judaism, I call on his life, spirit and experiences. All of his memories live on through me. My grandpa Abe came out of that soul-crushing experience in the camps with more soul than ever. He grew ever more firm in his convictions and outlook, a philosophy and way of being that he passed on to me. I have a positive outlook on life just as he did. And I believe that every person is equal, every person is important and every person is special. He taught me this.

"I have a very strong Jewish spirit and beautiful heart because he instilled that spirit in me throughout my childhood. How could he not? I saw his beautiful heart all the time. It was filled with love for others, his family and especially for my grandma Freida. I love others as he did—open-hearted, arms wide open. You could always feel and see the deep love my grandparents

shared. They, in turn, passed this amazing gift on to my mom, which she shares with me and my dad and the larger family.

"When my grandparents celebrated their fiftieth wedding anniversary, I wrote this tribute: "Grandma and Grandpa, you are like a single rose made of two colors, red and yellow, which stands perfectly straight in a vase made of gold. The red represents the deep love you have for each other, the yellow symbolizes the friendship you share because you keep giving to each other. The stem reflects your strength in overcoming hardships and the gold vase represents your solid, enduring marriage.

"I loved my grandpa and grandma beyond words. They hold a special place in my heart and will be with me forever."

William do Carmo, familiarly known as Bill Carmo, returned home to New Bedford from the Korean War in the late 1950s and settled in on Pleasant Street. One of his first stops was Abe Landau's tailor shop, just five blocks away, for he needed some civilian clothes. While he was being measured, the two men struck up a conversation.

"He wanted to know about me," Bill laughed. "Because he knew I had just returned from the military. So I told him about me and he told me the story of the camps and what happened to his family. In spite of his suffering, he still had great feeling for mankind—this tied us together."

Bill is the former president of the NAACP and remains active in civil rights. "Jewish people and black people have a lot in common," he says. "Man can do so many destructive things and so many good things. I am a historian of mankind, in my way, and Abe was too, and so we talked—about the Greeks, the Romans, about slavery. We talked inside the shop, outside the shop, we talked sitting on a bench—it was a conversation that went on for many decades.

"Abe wanted to know my connection to Jewish people, and that goes back to my childhood. As a kid, I lived on South First Street and worked around the neighborhood. Many Jewish people owned stores on South Water Street and I worked for all of them—delivering groceries, plucking chickens, selling newspapers. I was always on the move. Abe loved these stories. He couldn't believe I did all these things and went to school too."

After college, Bill put his many talents to use in construction and real estate, taking on some million-dollar projects including schools, apartments and transportation systems. Still, he recalls with a laugh, "I have to say that building a house for Abe and Freida was one of my more interesting challenges." Abe and Freida had decided to move to the West End of New Bedford, near Buttonwood Park, closer to the synagogue. "I worked with my men on the house—this was the easy part. The more challenging part was the finishing because Freida was making the decisions. She picked an expensive wallpaper and my men papered one wall. When she walked in, she said they weren't doing it right, it was upside down.

"I explained that my crew were very experienced and had done it exactly like it was in the book and she said, no, it wasn't right. So we took it off and put it on upside down. Well, she didn't like it that way either. Up or down, she didn't like it. So we put it back the original way. Then she picked out a laminate for the kitchen counter and after it was installed, she didn't like it."

Bill laughed at the memory. "I absorbed the extra cost because I loved them so much. And Abe had made five or six suits for me. Over the years, our friendship just blossomed. When Abe began speaking publicly about the Holocaust, the invitations started coming in, many from around Boston, and he didn't know how to get there. He asked me to be his driver. Freida would make sandwiches and off we'd go."

Bill often visited Abe in the nursing home after his stroke in 1998. The two men sat together outside and continued their conversation. Abe could no longer speak, but the two long-time friends didn't need words.

The late Ed Rudnick of New Bedford wrote about his friendship with Abe in an essay he had hoped to refine for this book. "Abe was my friend," wrote Ed. "By coincidence we both arrived in New Bedford in the early 1950s—he as a resettled, displaced person from Germany and I as a textile engineer from Boston. At first we were just acquaintances but I gradually became closer to Abe and his beloved wife, Freida, until we ultimately developed a close friendship during his last years. Most of Abe's stories and anecdotes

The Holocaust Memorial monument was designed by University of Massachusetts Dartmouth professor Peter London, and the sculpture was created by UMD professor Eric Lintala (at right) and visiting artist Stacy Latt Savage (at work). Abe guided the construction at every stage. Here, at UMD, he chats with Reverend Edward Dufresne and Rabbi Barry Hartman, while the artist etches his Auschwitz brand below the replica's wrist.

Landau Family Collection

I got directly from him during our numerous visits and while working together to create the Holocaust Memorial in New Bedford.

"In his later years, Abe Landau and other Holocaust survivors in this region reminded the Jewish community that there was no special place for families of Holocaust victims to go and say memorial prayers for their loved ones; there were no graves or tombstones for those who died during that horrible time. So Abe and others arranged for the Jewish Federation of Greater New Bedford, together with Tifereth Israel and Ahavath Achim synagogues to erect a special memorial for this purpose in the midst of New Bedford's Jewish cemetery. Besides being used for such memorial prayers year round, an annual Holocaust memorial was held at this cemetery just prior to the High Holy Days. Until his incapacity and ultimate passing in 2000, Cantor Abe Landau magnificently sang the special El Moleh Rachamin memorial prayer here in memory of the six million Jewish Holocaust victims, especially the ninety-five members of his own family."

The memorial in the Jewish cemetery was lovely but the cemetery was remote and not visible to most citizens of the area. Abe Landau wanted more. He wanted a Holocaust memorial that could be seen by local passersby. He wanted one that would reach out and grab them. He wanted a memorial that called on people to remember.

Abe's dearest friend, Edward Rudnick (second left), with monument designer Peter London and Freida, help break ground for the Holocaust Memorial Monument, 1998.

"He wanted a magnificent and unique Holocaust memorial in a most solemn and prominent area of Buttonwood Park, the city's premier park," said Ed Rudnick. Abe, Ed and others decided to appeal to the community. They arranged several meetings with past and present mayors, city councilors, park board members, and state and national representatives. For two years the ardent group worked tirelessly until, at last, the project was complete.

The Holocaust Memorial was erected in May 1998 in New Bedford's historic Buttonwood Park under the auspices of the Holocaust Education Committee of the Jewish Federation of Greater New Bedford.

The hand and number are modeled after Abe Landau. The pedestal lists 27 of the more infamous concentration camps. A dedication to the millions of victims appears on the slabs in Hebrew and English.

Peter London, co-chair of the Holocaust Education Committee, explained the difficulty of carrying out such a complex project as the Buttonwood Park Holocaust Memorial. "Originally when we approached the Jewish community, there was not much enthusiasm for the sculpture. There is a profound humiliation in Jewish history for us to have suffered this way. It was a betrayal by the western world, and, at first, there was a shunning of survivors by the Jewish community. American Jews were too eager to forget. At this point, the Jews were not yet ready to call attention to what happened. Not yet. But Fred Kalisz, the Polish mayor, was all for it. So was former mayor Rosemary Tierney and the former president of the UMD, Peter Cressy. And the non-Jewish community supported it. Abe himself always felt strongly that he wanted to work with the non-Jewish community as well as Jews.

"I came to know the Landaus after I had drawn a series of Holocaust victims. In my mind, I saw image after image and there was no rescue, their fate was to die. I drew them, their haunting faces. I had this bold idea to show the drawings to Abe and Freida. I wondered if they could see themselves there. I went over with my portfolio and our friendship began.

"I think Abe is a distinctly important man of our time. He added to our appreciation of all the lessons derived from the Holocaust. He was a major teacher, a great teacher. And the memorial is not just for Jews. He saw in it a universal lesson. Abe went below the surface, he dug deep and held tight to memory. He was un-American in this way, in the sense that we Americans skirt the surface of things and don't go below. Gravitas comes from not relinquishing your history. Abe lived his history, spoke his history."

The monument, designed by Peter London, is striking. It features a forearm and hand jutting toward the heavens. The number on the forearm reads 141282, Abe's number. "In the monument Abe is not shaking his fist at God. It's more in prayerfulness, supplication, the hand rising, resilience, suffering, smoke ascending, incense, prayer. It's subtle, psychological," said Peter London.

Abe and Freida's favorite photo—on a bench in front of the Holocaust Monument at Buttonwood Park, 1998. - Landau Family Collection

In the New Bedford Public Library, on a wall lined with portraits of local notables, hangs an oil painting of Abraham Landau by portrait artist Deborah Macy. It is part of her series on Contemporary Role Models, and she chose Abe Landau because he represents morality: "He is the flesh-and-blood personification of suffering and survival, yet without cynicism. It's a miracle! He is a loving, joyous man of faith."

Abe Landau died on January 7, 2000 at the New Bedford Jewish Convalescent Home at age 77. His beloved Freida died at their daughter's home four months later, on Yom HaShoah, the day of remembrance for the Holocaust. Abe and Freida were married for fifty-four years and they lived many lives. They are now at peace. Their incredible journey is over.

A note left at the base of the Holocaust Monument, 1998.

Landau Family Collection

During the evacuation and liquidation of Auschwitz in January 1945, almost all important documents of the camp were destroyed, including prisoners' personal files. Fortunately, the Office for Information on Former Prisoners at the Auschwitz-Birkenau State Museum was able to produce a partially saved record of Abe Landau's internment. From this particular document, we learn that the five-foot-one-inch Polish Jew from Wilczyn was arrested in Zagórów for "Anti-Nazi activity." His parents are Jakob and Gitla (nee Buchner). He is a tailor, unmarried, with a 7th-grade education. His hair is red; his oblong face droops; he has 7 teeth missing and (not surprisingly) gaps between what's left. His crime record? "Alledgedly None."

KonzentrationslagerAUSCHWITZ   Art der Haft: *Sch. Jude*   Gef. Nr.: *141282*

Name und Vorname: *Landau Abram* Israel   (3231)

geb.: *25.6.1922* zu: *Wilczyn, Kr. Konin*

Wohnort: *Zagorów, Hindenburg i.f. Kr. v.o*

Beruf: *Schneider*   Rel.: *mos*

Staatsangehörigkeit: *ehem. Polen*   Stand: *led*

Name der Eltern: *Jakob u. Gitla, geb. Buchner*   Rasse: *jüd*

Wohnort: *B. in Haft*

Name der Ehefrau: /   Rasse: /

Wohnort:

Kinder: *keine* Alleiniger Ernährer der Familie oder der Eltern: /

Vorbildung: *7 Kl. Volksschule*

Militärdienstzeit: /   von — bis   /

Kriegsdienstzeit: von — bis

Grösse: *1.55*   Nase: *gnadl.* Haare: *rötlich* Gestalt: *schlank*

Mund: *normal* Bart: *keinen* Gesicht: *längt* Ohren: *normal*

Sprache: *poln.*   Augen: *braun* Zähne: *lück 7 fehle*

Ansteckende Krankheit oder Gebrechen: *keine*

Besondere Kennzeichen: *keine*

Rentenempfänger: *nein*

Verhaftet am: *20.8.41*   wo: *in Zagorów*

1. Mal eingeliefert: *26. Aug. 1943*   2. Mal eingeliefert:

Einweisende Dienststelle: **RSHA.**

Grund:

Parteizugehörigkeit: *keine*   von — bis

Welche Funktionen: *keine*

Mitglied v. Unterorganisationen: *nein*

Kriminelle Vorstrafen: *angebl. keine*

Politische Vorstrafen: *angebl. keine*

Ich bin darauf hingewiesen worden, dass meine Bestrafung wegen intellektueller Urkundenfälschung erfolgt, wenn sich die obigen Angaben als falsch erweisen sollten.

v. g. u. *Landau Abram*   **Der Lagerkommandant**

25. VI. 1922

KL/42 4.43 500.000   *5*

136

ENDNOTES

Introduction

1. I. G. Farben and Degussa owned most of Degesch Limited, the company that actually produced Zyklon B, which had been around since the 1920s and used as a pesticide. In early 1942, Zyklon B was the preferred extermination tool of the Nazi regime, claiming the lives of roughly 1.2 million people, mostly Jews, in the Auschwitz, Majdanek and Sachsenhausen camps. [Wikipedia]

Chapter I

1. The *ba'al koreh* is a Jewish official who reads the Torah in the synagogue. Literally it means "master of reading."
2. Though Ashkenazim literally means "German Jews," the term applies to most Jews of central or eastern Europe. More than 80 percent of Jews today are Ashkenazi. They preserve Palestinian rather than Babylonian Jewish traditions, and some still use Yiddish. Although Abe Landau practiced orthodox faith more akin to Haredi or Sephardic tradition, ethnically he was considered Ashkenazi. [Jewish Virtual Library]
3. A *yarmulke* is the traditional cap that covers the top of the head, fulfilling the Jewish requirement that the head be covered at all times.
4. A *shtreimel* is a circular hat made of fur usually worn only by married Jewish men.
5. A pogrom is an organized massacre of a targeted ethnic group, in particular that of Jews in Russia or eastern Europe. It is often characterized by rioting, murder and destruction of property. Its origin is Russian, literally "devastation." [Oxford Dictionary]

Chapter II

1. *Volksdeutsche* is the term used by the Nazis for ethnic Germans living outside the Reich. The Volksdeutsche could be effectively mobilized by the Nazis to terrorize occupied populations, disseminate propaganda, and help expand German nationalism and racial superiority throughout central Europe. By contrast, ethnic Germans living inside the Reich were *Reichsdeutsche*. [Wikipedia]
2. The Hitler Youth (*Hitlerjugend*), 1922–1945, was started as a Youth League but was transformed into a paramilitary wing of the Nazi Party whose purpose was to indoctrinate youth in Nazism and prepare them for military service by familiarizing them with weapons and basic tactics. In 1925, when the Nazi Party had been refounded, the membership grew to over 5,000, and by 1930, it had enlisted over 25,000 boys aged 14 and upwards. After 1936, when membership became mandatory for Aryans, its ranks grew rapidly. Throughout the 1940s, when most every youth group in Germany was absorbed into the Hitler Youth, membership swelled into the tens of millions. Wearing uniforms and carrying ranks similar to those of the SS, the Hitlerjugend was tapped for military service as the war spiraled out of control. By 1945, virtually every young male in Germany was, in some way, connected to the Hitlerjugend.
3. The Nazis' random roundup of citizens was called *lapanka* by Poles, after a children's game similar to "tag."
4. The SS was formed in 1925 under the name "*Saal-Schutz*" (Assembly Hall Protection), intended for providing security for Nazi party meetings and as a personal protection squad for Adolf Hitler. Led by Heinrich Himmler between 1929 and 1945, the SS was renamed to "Schutz-Staffel" and grew from a small paramilitary formation to one of the largest and most powerful organizations in the Third Reich. Members were selected according to the Nazi ideology, creating elite police and military units such as the Waffen-SS. Hitler used the SS to form an order of men claimed to be superior in racial purity and ability to other Germans and national groups.

   Chosen to implement the "Final Solution," the SS was the lead branch in carrying out the killing, torture and enslavement of approximately twelve million people. Most victims were Jews or of Slavic extraction, as well as Roma (Gypsies) and those viewed as threats to "race hygiene" or Nazi ideology—including the mentally or physically handicapped, homosexuals, or political dissidents. After 1945, the SS and the Nazi Party were designated as criminal organizations. [Wikipedia]
5. In pre-war Poland, Jewish homes were often identified by a *Mezuzah*, a small parchment scroll bearing biblical verses, which is attached to the right of the door post.
6. *Krystallnacht* means "night of broken glass," so called because of the glass littering the streets from shattered storefront windows. It is believed that Krystallnacht was organized by the Nazis, though they claim it was a spontaneous reaction to the murder of a German diplomat. In any case, German police and military did not intervene with the pogroms. In fact, in many cases, they assisted.

Chapter III

1. Abe may have exaggerated this number. As there were only about 150 Jews in Wilczyn, 200 horse-drawn wagons would provide far more steerage than was needed to transport them. However, it's also possible that Wilczyn was a collection center for residents of *shtetls* (small Jewish villages in eastern Europe), and Jews were brought here before being transported to the ghetto in Zagórów.
2. Mieczysław Sękiewicz's chilling testimony is from *Chelmno: A Small Village in Europe* by Shmuel Krakowski. An excerpt can be found on Leon Jedwab's website, http://www.leonjedwab.com/leonjedwab/kb_testimony.html. A Polish veterinary doctor, Sękiewicz first testified before a judical Polish Committee on October 27, 1945 and again in June 1968 for the Polish Committee Investigating the Nazi Crimes in Poznań. Dr. Sękiewicz describes the horrific massacre that he was forced to take part in at Kazimierz Biskupi.

Chapter IV

1. In Nazi Germany, the principal camps were designated *"Arbeitslager"* (Labor Camp), *"Arbeitserziehungslager"* (Labor Education Camp), and *"Zwangsarbeitslager für Juden"* (Forced Labor Camps for Jews). All of these camps existed in the Inowrocław region and were run by the regional headquarters of the State Police.

   Forced Labor Camps for Jews first appeared in 1938 inside the Reich and later in Eastern and Southern Europe. Initially, they were not of primary economic significance but were mainly characterized by pointless activities meant to humiliate and humble the victims. With the rising demand for manpower in the defense industry, the economic utilization of Jewish labor became more important. This form of exploitation did not override the fundamental objective of the National Socialists—the elimination of Jews; at best, it meant a timely postponement of their murder.

   Nazi labor education camps (Arbeitserziehungslagers), were introduced in 1939 and aimed to serve local industry or to discipline a workforce and oppress resistance. Officially, Arbeitserziehungslagers were used to imprison German laborers with terms of 21 to 56 days, though many stayed longer. Because of the short prison terms, intense cruelty was administered to terrorize prisoners and crush their spirit. The Arbeitserziehungslagers were also used as places of execution by the Gestapo. By 1940, as the war progressed, these camps served no "educational" purpose and were dominated by Eastern European civilian laborers and prisoners of war, making them indistinguishable from forced labor camps (Zwangsarbeitslagers). At that time, there were only eight labor education camps, but by the end of the war there were 200 camps within the Reich imprisoning half a million people.

   At Zwangsarbeitslagers, through hard physical labor, disastrous living conditions, torture and death, the Nazis hoped for a fast and permanent repressive effect on the living and working demeanor of the prisoners. The difference between these forced labor camps and concentration camps—places of mass extermination where people were systematically slaughtered—became less distinguishable through the course of the war, as the National Socialist annihilation policy kept radicalizing. The forced labor camps for Jews, therefore, became places of "extermination through labor," as evidenced by the high death rate. [The German Federal Archives]

2. *Wehrmacht* was the name given to Nazi Germany's armed forces from 1935 to 1945. It was made up of three branches—the Heer (army), Kriegsmarine (navy), and Luftwaffe (air force). More than 18.2 million men and women served the Wehrmacht during its time. The Waffen-SS, the combat branch of the SS (the Nazi Party's paramilitary organization), became the de facto fourth branch of the Wehrmacht as it expanded from three regiments to 38 divisions by 1945. Although the SS was autonomous and existed alongside the Wehrmacht, the Waffen-SS field units were placed under the operational control of the Supreme High Command of the Armed Forces (Oberkommando der Wehrmacht, OKW). [The World War II Multimedia Database; Encyclopedia Brittanica]

Chapter V

1. Kapos were inmates who supervised prisoners in the camps. They functioned as camp police and enforcers, carrying out the will of the Nazi camp commandants and guards. They often behaved as brutally as their rigid SS bosses, dispensing harsh punishment, degradation and murder to prisoners. Some kapos were Jewish, with little empathy for their fellow Jews. Others were convicted murderers, thugs and hardened criminals of any nationality.

   Kapos were involved in all aspects of prisoner administration and had many responsibilities, such as implementing commands, maintaining order, leading work groups, determining the health of inmates and ensuring that workers performed tasks and met quotas. If an order was not fulfilled, the kapo in charge was directly responsible. Failure to perform these duties resulted in severe punishment and even death.

   If a person was selected to be a kapo, he or she had no choice but to take the position. It was a matter of survival. Kapos enjoyed their own reserved section in the prison barrack, had plenty to eat, and well clothed.

   Upon Liberation, many kapos were chased down by other inmates and killed while the liberators watched. After the war, kapos were charged as war criminals, as many viewed their actions as a form of complicity. Their prosecution, particularly those who were Jewish, created an ethical dilemma which continues to this day. [The Jewish Virtual Library, The Holocaust Documentation and Education Center]

2. The Gestapo was the German internal security police force under the administration of the SS and Heinrich Himmler, Chief of German Police. It had the authority to investigate cases of treason, espionage, sabotage and criminal attacks on the Nazi Party and Germany. In 1936, a law was passed giving the Gestapo authority to operate without judicial oversight. As one SS officer stated, "As long as the police carry out the will of the leadership, it is acting legally." The Gestapo was responsibe for setting up and administering concentration camps. It also supplied staff to the Einsatzgruppen, the SS paramilitary death squads that were responsible for the mass shootings of Jews and other undesirables. During the war, the Gestapo expanded to around 46,000 members. [Encyclopedia Brittanica]

Chapter VI

3. The Auschwitz Calendarium reports that on August 27th, 1943, a group of 1,026 Jews arrived in Auschwitz, brought there by the Reich Security Main Office from "Zwangsarbeiterlager für Juden Wollstein" (Forced Labor Camp for Jews in Wolsztyn) in Poznań province. Of these men (Abe among them), 1,016 received numbers from 140721 to 141736. The ten other men were killed in the gas chambers. From the memoir, "The Dentist of Auschwitz," we learn that this train transport stopped in Gutenbrunn, Płaszów, Czestochowa, Katowice, and other stops, taking at least four days to reach Auschwitz. Abe would have boarded in either Gleiwitz or Katowice. [Office for Information on Former Prisoners, Auschwitz-Birkenau State Museum]

4. Tattooing was introduced in Auschwitz in 1941, when numbers written on clothes became impractical due to the rate at which prisoners died and swapped clothes. Tattooing was deemed the best way to identify the bodies of the dead. Originally, tattoos were applied by a numerical needle-punch which could create a number-shaped wound in a single blow; into which ink would then be rubbed. Later, a single-needle tattoo device was considered more practical. Several numerical series were introduced from 1941 until 1945 to distinguish a prisoner's race, gender, and nationality—each new series beginning with the number "1." Some Jewish prisoners were also branded with a triangle, though not all. Auschwitz was the only camp to tattoo prisoners. [United States Holocaust Memorial Museum]

5. Musselmann is a German term (pl. Muselmänner; in Polish Muzułman; pronounced moozleman) used among concentration camp inmates to refer to prisoners who were near death due to starvation, exhaustion or hopelessness. Identifiable by their physical and psycho-logical decline—emaciated, lethargic and indifferent to their surroundings, not able stand up for more than a few seconds—musselmanner had no chance for survival and were readily exterminated. Generally, other prisoners stayed clear of musselmanner in fear of contracting the condition.

   The term "musselmänn" was first used at Auschwitz-Birkenau and spread to other concentration camps. Its literal translation is "Muslim," though, ironically, it was applied mostly to Jews. Some scholars believe the term originated from the similarity between the crouching position of a person dying of hunger and that of a Muslim in a traditional praying position. According to Giorgio Agamben in *Remnants of Auschwitz: The Witness and the Archive,* the term connotes the complete surrender that is the literal meaning behind the Arabic word Islam: The musselmann is one who has surrendered all hope, all dignity, and thus, nearly all humanity.

   > [The Musselmann] was a destroyed man/woman, a victim of gradual extermination…[who] made mechanic movements with no reason.…The "Musselmann" perished because he could not go on. He was the symbol for mass-dying, a death of hunger, of being left alone, of killing the soul, a living corpse.…

   Agamben suggests that musselmanner are the true witnesses of the camps even though they cannot speak. He calls them the "anonymous mass" that formed the "back-bone of the camps." [Shoah Resource Center, Yad Vashem; Wikipedia]

6. A lazarett is a small German military hospital or clinic usually found on a military base or prison camp. The lazarett also served as a lab for experiments.

Chapter X Buna

1. The *Talmud* is a central text for mainstream Judaism, consisting of a record of rabbinic discussions pertaining to Jewish customs, philosophy, history, law, and ethics. While the Talmud contains both oral and written scriptures, it is the most significant collection of the Jewish oral tradition interpreting the Torah. The "Oral Torah" is a tradition explaining what the scriptures mean and how to interpret

An identification card designating that Abe Landau was a political prisoner at Auschwitz. - Landau Family Collection

them. Orthodox Jews believe God taught the Oral Torah to Moses, and he taught it to others, down to the present day. This tradition was maintained only in oral form until about the second century when the oral law was compiled and written down in a document called the *Mishnah.* Over the next few centuries, additional commentaries elaborating on the Mishnah, known as the *Gemara,* were written down in Jerusalem and Babylon. The Gemara and the Mishnah together form the Talmud. The Baby-lonian Talmud is more comprehensive, and is the one most people mean if they just say "the Talmud" without specifying which one. It was completed in the 5th century. [from Judaism 101, online encyclopedia of Judaism]

2. Alhough many men, women, and children died of exhaus-tion or froze to death during the marches, a far greater number were killed by the SS guards who shot or beat to death anyone lagging behind. Estimates of the number of people who died during the Auschwitz death marches range from 9,000 to 15,000. [Wollheim Memorial]

Chapter XII

1. The UN and the Jewish Distribution Center form "The Jewish Joint Distribution Committee (JDC)." The JDC is the world's leading Jewish humanitarian assistance organization, working in more than 70 countries to alle-viate hunger and hardship, rescue Jews in danger, create lasting connections to Jewish life, and provide immediate relief and long-term developmental support for victims of natural and man-made disasters. [from the JDC website]

INDEX

BIBLIOGRAPHY

Books and Periodicals

Höss, Rudolf, and Steven. Paskuly. *Death Dealer: The Memoirs of the SS Commandant at Auschwitz*. New York: Da Capo Press, 1996.

Jacobs, Benjamin. *The Dentist of Auschwitz: A Memoir*. Lexington: University Press of Kentucky, 1995.

Krakowski, Shmuel. *Chelmno A Small Village in Europe: The First Nazi Mass Extermination Camp*. Yerushalayim: Yad Vashem, 2001.

Laqueur, Walter, and Judith Tydor Baumel-Schwartz. *The Holocaust Encyclopedia*. New Haven: Yale Univ. Press, 2001.

Megargee, Geoffrey P. *The United States Holocaust Memorial Museum Encyclopedia of Camps and Ghettos, 1933-1945*. Bloomington: Indiana University Press in association with the United States Holocaust Memorial Museum, 2009.

Agamben, Giorgio. *Remnants of Auschwitz: The Witness and the Archive*. New York: Zone Books, 2000.

Nyiszli, Miklós. *Auschwitz: A Doctor's Eyewitness Account*. New York [Boston]: Arcade Pub. Distributed by Little, Brown, and Co., 1993.

Rhodes, Richard. *Masters of Death: The SS-Einsatzgruppen and the Invention of the Holocaust*. New York: A.A. Knopf, 2002.

Wiesel, Elie, and Marion. Wiesel. *The Night Trilogy: Night; Dawn; Day / Elie Wiesel*. New York: Hill and Wang, 2008.

Internet Articles and Archive Information, Last Accessed September 2011.

Auschwitz Museum Archives and State Museum Auschwitz-Birkenau. "Office for Information about Former Prisoners." http://en.auschwitz.org.pl/m/index.php?option=com_content&task=view&Itemid=31&id=530

Auschwitz-Brkenau Memorial & Museum. "KL Auschwitz-Birkenau" http://en.auschwitz.org.pl/h/index.php?option=com_content&task=view&id=27&Itemid=1.

Buchenwald and Mittlebau-Dora Memorial Foundations. http://www.buchenwald.de/english/ and http://www.dora.de/index.php?id=148&l=1.

Bundesarchives. "The Digital Picture Archives of the Federal Archives." http://www.bild.bundesarchiv.de/

Bundesarchives / EVZ Foundation. "Overview Directories of Places of Detention." http://www.bundesarchiv.de/zwangsarbeit/haftstaetten/index.php.en?tab=1.

———. "Types of Camps." http://www.bundesarchiv.de/zwangsarbeit/haftstaetten/index.php.en?tab=2.

Encyclopedia Brittanica Online. http://www.britannica.com/.

Familie Tenhumberg. "1933-1945 Lager und Haftstätten." http://www.tenhumbergreinhard.de/05aaff9bed0fa4003/index.html.

Ghetto Fighters House Museum. "Archives." http://www.gfh.org.il/Eng/

Historia Harcerstwa Prawobrzeznego Posnania (Seeking the true history of Poznan) "In Occupied Poznan." http://www.historiahpnm.jdm.pl/index.php/w-okupowanym-poznaniu.

History Wiz. http://www.historywiz.com/camp.htm.

The Holocaust Documentation and Education Center. http://holocausteducation.wetpaint.com/.

Holocaust Education & Archive Research Team. "Buchenwald Concentration Camp." http://www.holocaustresearchproject.org/othercamps/buchenwald.html.

———. "The Auschwitz Protocol." http://www.holocaustresearchproject.org/othercamps/auschproto2.html.

———. "The Łódź Ghetto, 1940-1944." http://www.holocaustresearchproject.org/ghettos/Lodz/lodzghetto.html.

International Tracing Service of the Red Cross. http://www.its-arolsen.org/en/homepage/index.html.

Jedwab, Leon. "My Journey Through the Holocaust." http://www.leonjedwab.com/leonjedwab/Home.html.

The Jewish Historical Institute. http://www.jewishinstitute.org.pl/en/home/index/0.htm.

The Jewish Virtaul Library. "Nordhausen (Dora-Mittelbau)." http://www.jewishvirtuallibrary.org/jsource/ Holocaust/Nordtoc.html. Also, various articles from "The Holocaust." http://www.jewishvirtuallibrary.org/ jsource/holo.html.

JewishGen.org. Various articles and "Holocaust Period." http://www.shtetlinks.jewishgen.org/Zaglembie/Zag006c.html.

Kujawsko Pomorskie - Szlaki Pamięci (Kuyavia and Pomerania - Memory Pathways). "Niemiecki obóz na Błoniu… (The German camp at Inowrocław-Blonie…)." http://szlakipamieci.kujawsko-pomorskie.pl/index. php?option=com_content&view=article&id=79&Itemid=96.

Lexicon der Wehrmacht. "Standort Montwy." http://www.lexikon-der-wehrmacht.de/Kasernen/Wehrkreis21/ KasernenMontwy-R.htm.

The Mazal Library. http://www.mazal.org/Default.htm.

Memoire Juive et Education (Jewish Education and Memory). "Le camp de Dora." http://d-d.natanson.pagesperso-orange.fr/dora.htm .

Museum of the History of Polish Jews. http://www.jewishmuseum.org.pl/en/cms/home-page/.

The National Ex-Prisoner of War Association. http://www.prisonerofwar.org.uk/.

The Nizkor Project. "The Holocaust Web Project," and various articles. http://www.nizkor.org/fast-track.shtml.

The Pegasus Archive. "The British Airborne Forces, 1940-1945." http://www.pegasusarchive.org/.

Poland National Digital Archives (NAC). "NAC Collections Online." http://www.audiovis.nac.gov.pl/search/.

Scrapbookpages.com. "Buchenwald Concentration Camp." http://www.scrapbookpages.com/buchenwald/.

Stadt Ellrich. "The outskirts of Ellrich-Juliushutte." http://www.stadtellrich.de/texte/seite.php?id=55256.

Tauber Holocaust Library. http://www.tauberholocaustlibrary.org/.

United States Holocaust Memorial Museum. "Auschwitz." Holocaust Encyclopedia. http://www.ushmm.org/wlc/ en/article.php?ModuleId=10005189.

_____. "Dora-Mittelbau." Holocaust Encyclopedia. http://www.ushmm.org/wlc/en/article. php?ModuleId=10005322.

_____. "Jewish Community of Kalisz in the Interwar Years." Holocaust Encyclopedia. http://www.ushmm.org/ wlc/en/article.php?ModuleId=10005789.

_____. "The Holocaust." Holocaust Encyclopedia. http://www.ushmm.org/wlc/en/article.php?ModuleId=10005189.

_____. Bedzin. Photo Archives. http://digitalassets.ushmm.org/photoarchives/detail.aspx?id=1084190&search=D ER&index=521. Also, other articles.

Virtual Shtetl. "Towns," various town histories and articles. http://www.sztetl.org.pl/en/selectcity/.

Wartime Press. http://www.wartimepress.com/archives.asp?TID=Illustrierter%20Beobachter%20 1939&MID=Illustrierter%20Beobachter&q=284&FID=274.

Wikipedia. "Buna-Werke." http://de.wikipedia.org/wiki/Buna-Werke.

_____ "Auschwitz concentration camp." http://en.wikipedia.org/wiki/Auschwitz. Also, other references.

Wollheim Memorial. "Abandoning the Auschwitz Camp Complex: The Death March." http://www.wollheim-memorial.de/en/raeumung_des_lagerkomplexes_auschwitz_der_todesmarsch.

_____ "Death Marches and Liberation of the Auschwitz Concentration Camp." http://www.wollheim-memorial. de/en/todesmaersche_und_befreiung_des_kz_auschwitz. Also, other articles.

The World War II Multimedia Database. http://worldwar2database.com/

Yad Vashem. "Digital Collections." http://www1.yadvashem.org/yv/en/resources/index.asp.

_____ "The Auschwitz Album." http://www1.yadvashem.org/exhibitions/album_Auschwitz/intro.html.

Acknowledgments / Credits

This memoir is based, in large part, on a series of interviews conducted in 1982 and 1983 by Professors Yale Magrass and Robert Michael of the University of Massachusetts Dartmouth. The two men were contracted by the Jewish Federation of Greater New Bedford to interview Abe Landau to record his personal memoir for publication. It is through the generosity of the Landau family and the Jewish Federation of Greater New Bedford that we are able to fulfill Abe's dream by rendering his story into book format. We are grateful to Professor Magrass and the late Professor Michael for their work, and to the University of Massachusetts Dartmouth for its cooperation in supplying additional materials.

Many individuals contributed mightily to this volume. In particular, Abe Landau's daughter Ann, granddaughter Lauren, and son-in-law Dennis, made it happen because of their generosity, graciousness and determination. The vision and conviction of Abe's dear friend, the late Eddie Rudnick, was crucial to our involvement in the project at the outset in 2001. We also acknowledge the critical role of Mary Schwartz, past president of The Jewish Federation of Greater New Bedford, who encouraged Abe to record his story and enlisted the Federation's support.

We want to thank the contributing editors, Karen Gravel and Catherine McLaughlin, for the hundreds of hours they spent listening to tapes and then rendering them into a cohesive story. We thank Claire Nemes, Heather Haggerty, Eric Pacy, Jarosław Buziak and Robert Waxler for their editorial, research, writing and administrative assistance. We are also grateful to Marsha Onufrak and Cindy Yoken for the time and resources they have invested and for their involvement in fundraising and the development of an education component to be implemented in secondary schools; and because they held our hands along the way and never let us down. Finally, we're grateful to everyone at the Jewish Federation of Greater New Bedford, particularly Olga Yorish and Jim Wilcox, for facilitating our efforts from start to finish.

Editors

Jay Avila
Marsha L. McCabe
Joseph D. Thomas

Contributing Editors

Karen Gravel
Heather Haggerty
Catherine McLaughlin
Claire Nemes
Eric Pacy

Other Contributors

Jarosław Buziak
Ruth Caswell
Elizabeth Comeau
Tracy Furtado
Dariusz Goiński
Marcin Habel
Leon Jedwab & Family
Ann & Dennis Kantor
Lauren Joy Kantor-Finger
Sean Lloyd
Yale Magrass
Robert McCabe
Robert Michael
Marsha Onufrak
Ed Rudnick
Mary Schwartz
Robert Waxler
John Whoriskey
Cynthia Yoken

Resources

Auschwitz-Birkenau
    State Museum
Buchenwald and Dora-Mittlebau
    Memorial Foundation
German Federal Archives
Ghetto Fighters House Archives
Jewish Federation of
    Greater New Bedford
Polish National Digital Archives
Poznań Society of Friends of
    Sciences
The Standard-Times
Time Magazine
United States Holocaust
    Memorial Museum
University of Massachusetts
    Dartmouth
USC Shoah Foundation Institute
Virtual Shtetl
Yad Vashem Archives